A CUBAN REFUGEE'S JOURNEY
TO THE AMERICAN DREAM

WELL HOUSE BOOKS

# A CUBAN REFUGEE'S JOURNEY TO THE AMERICAN DREAM

*The Power of Education*

Gerardo M. González

Indiana University Press

This book is a publication of

Indiana University Press
Office of Scholarly Publishing
Herman B Wells Library 350
1320 East 10th Street
Bloomington, Indiana 47405 USA

iupress.indiana.edu

Manufactured in the United States of America

Cataloging information is available from the Library of Congress.

ISBN 978-0-253-03700-8 (hdbk.)
ISBN 978-0-253-03555-4 (pbk.)
ISBN 978-0-253-03556-1 (e-bk.)

2 3 4 5   23 22 21 20 19 18

*To my parents*
*Elio Angel González and Armantina*
*González Torres*
*For their love and sacrifices*

# Contents

# Acknowledgments

I GRATEFULLY ACKNOWLEDGE and thank the many wonderful people who have contributed to the preparation of this memoir. First of all, I thank my parents Elio Angel González and Armantina González Torres for their love, guidance, and support throughout the years. They contributed many stories and anecdotes that helped shape this book, and provided insightful perspectives on our lives as Cuban refugees and on the values I hold as a Cuban-American educator. To my sister Maritza, who helped me fill in some blanks in my memory and provided a photographic history of our family, which she meticulously organized over the years. Maritza, you have always been there for me. I love you, and many thanks.

To my wife and partner, Marjorie, who always found a way to kindly let me know when my vanity was getting in the way of my writing, and who enriched this book through her patience, devotion, and thoughtful comments: I express my love and thanks. My love and thanks also go to my children Justin, Jarrett, Ian, and Julie, who encouraged and supported me throughout this process.

To the people mentioned in this book, including Hugo Morales, Rafael Garcia, Oscar (Tommy) Pedraja, Arturo Saviñon, Rolando Breto, Richard Swanson, Carol Van Hartesveldt, Harold Riker, Governor Otis Bowen, Charlie Reed, Joe Wittmer, David Smith, Rod McDavis, Ken Gros Louis, and the many, many others named and unnamed, who have touched my life in so many positive ways: I say thanks.

Of course, the loving memories of my paternal grandparents Manuel González Méndez and Encarnación de la Cruz Soto, as well as my aunt Luisa Peralta, were never far from my thoughts while writing this memoir.

Many thanks also go to Lee Ann Sandweiss, who wrote a story about my first trip to Cuba for *Bloom Magazine*, and encouraged me to write a book. Her guidance and editorial assistance through the proposal preparation process were invaluable. Likewise, I'm grateful to Gary Dunham, director of Indiana University Press, who also provided helpful suggestions during the early stages of writing. Special thanks also to Robert Clark, Jenny Ashton, Alan Gold and Sandra Balonyi for their terrific input and excellent editorial suggestions. Additional editorial services were provided by Jan R. Holloway, whose contributions significantly improved the manuscript and helped me put it all together. For cover design and art direction, I acknowledge the fine work of the IU Press team and Lee Griffin.

This book is a labor of love. It could not have been realized without the encouragement, support, and loving assistance of everyone named above, and many others who believed in me. My heartfelt thanks to you all.

I gratefully acknowledge the following sources for permission to reprint from previously published work:

GONZÁLEZ, GERARDO M. and CHARLES L. CARNEY. 2014. "Challenging the Spectacle: A Case Study on Education Policy Advocacy." *International Journal of Leadership and Change* 2 (1): 19–27. Copyright © WKU College of Education and Behavioral Sciences. All rights reserved. Used by permission of Dr. Joseph P. Cangemi, editor.

SANDWEISS, LEE ANN. 2012. "A Sentimental Journey." *Bloom Magazine* 7 (5): 114–119. © 2006–2015 Bloomington Magazine, Inc. All rights reserved. Used by permission of the author and Malcolm Abrams, publisher.

A CUBAN REFUGEE'S JOURNEY
TO THE AMERICAN DREAM

# Prologue

How many of us begin life not knowing who we are or where we live? How many children pass their childhood in a state of utter confusion, not able to speak the language of their neighborhood or understand the alien culture into which they've been thrust? How many children sit in a school classroom, taunted every day and viewed as dumb by their fellow students and teachers because they can't understand a word that's being said?

Life is confusing enough for a child—any child—but with the solid footing of a stable home and a family that is well integrated into society, most kids can negotiate their way through the joys of childhood and the traumas of being a teenager and build on these foundational years to become responsible adults. Given a solid home life, school, college, and the workforce can be natural progressions for many of us. We grow, we advance, and we achieve.

So what happens when a family's stable ground is suddenly ripped from under a child's feet and he feels like he's walking through quicksand? When he sees his father and mother not as successful adults but living in constant fear? What goes through his mind when he is forced to remain mute, day after day, year after year, because he is afraid if he speaks, his teachers will discipline him? When he becomes stuck, because his teachers interpret his silence as bad behavior?

These were the issues I faced as a boy of eleven. I was once a bright and happy child. But when my family relocated to a strange and forbidding society, I couldn't speak or understand those around me. I was forced to conform to the standards of a society I simply couldn't comprehend.

My name is Gerardo González. I am a Cuban refugee who arrived in the United States shortly after Fidel Castro came to power. We fled a regime we wanted no part of, whose economics and ideology we distrusted. But in the United States my father, mother, sister, and I suffered dislocation, isolation, and fear. Today's immigrants and refugees, in the main, face even more daunting challenges. Regardless of their reasons for fleeing and the traumas they suffer, all who find themselves stateless face common experiences.

This is my story, but it's also the story of all immigrants who have had to leave their homes out of fear and desperation. We share a constant fear of authority in everything we do. We feel isolated when we see people our own age, born in our host nation, walking freely along the pavement. We feel we're here under sufferance.

If the world is to survive today's refugee and migrant crisis, we have to remember what happened at the beginning of the last century, along the pathways etched into the fertile soil of a young America. We have to remember the time when people and governments saw refugees, migrants, and immigrants not as an unwelcome invasion or a drain on society but as a resource that, when nurtured, would become society's most valuable asset—its citizens.

This isn't a book about politics or the rights and wrongs of global disputes. This is a book about one person—a refugee, a boy whose childhood was ripped from him, yet who, thanks to a few caring people in the society where he grew up, became an adult who succeeded beyond anybody's wildest expectations. Decades ago, he cowered in a church in fear, pretending to be mute simply to escape punishment. No one could have predicted his future professional roles as teacher, advocate, professor, and dean of education at one of America's most prestigious universities. And now, by some extraordinary turn of fate, he is one of the leaders chosen to help foster a new relationship between Cuba, the nation from which he was exiled, and the United States, the nation that opened its arms to him.

I hope my story will resonate in the mind of every person who has been forcibly relocated because of war or disputes, religion, or territory or by governments who put ideology before the needs of their people. It's a story that goes beyond compassion to one of the fundamental human rights, a right to which every child is entitled. It's about what can change the life of a child, and indeed the world—the right to an education!

Education is more, much more, than learning to read, write, and do sums. Education is an investment in the greatest asset a nation possesses: its people. Education is the way to open minds and help people realize their potential. It provides the tools children need to establish themselves in society, to function and grow, to develop the skills that ultimately enable them to become full, valuable, and productive members of society. Let a nation invest in a person's education, then watch that investment return to that nation a thousandfold.

So let me begin at the end.

Let me take you back to where I lived until I was eleven, to the land of my birth, seeing sights and smells I hadn't experienced in a lifetime.

Only now can I immerse myself in the joy and pain of memory—a memory of a once-happy childhood in one of the most beautiful places on earth.

# 1 A Homecoming

As the plane approached the runway in Havana, my heart thudded at the sight of the royal palms, the national tree of Cuba, dotting the landscape. As a child going on road trips through the countryside, I was mesmerized by the beautiful trees that seemed to appear everywhere. The day was bright, hot, and humid—just as I remembered. I walked into the terminal at the José Martí airport in disbelief. It had been fifty years since I had touched Cuban soil!

The year is 2012. Unlike the day I left Cuba as a terrified eleven-year-old, I was returning not only as an adult but as a leader—a widely respected American educator. I was leading a group of alumni from my university who were among the first Americans to enter the tropical island since relations between the two countries began to improve under the Obama and Raúl Castro administrations.

Memories flooded back during the brief visit—some happy, but many bittersweet. I did not immediately realize that going back would bring about a deeper level of understanding of my parents' motivation for leaving Cuba and the experiences that have shaped my life.

Seemingly ordinary sights unleashed powerful memories and emotions. It was like stepping back in time. There are centuries-old ways of doing things in Cuba. Seeing a *bodega*, a small Cuban convenience store, for the first time as an adult was very emotional. As a child, I used to go to my grandfather's bodega to pick up things that my mother needed—rice, beans, eggs—or simply to visit with my grandfather. On his way home from the bodega each night, my grandfather would bring me small pieces of chocolate, cheeses, and other treats he knew I enjoyed.

My family was among the many thousands of Cubans who left the island for the United States between the January 1959 Fidel Castro takeover and the Cuban missile crisis of October 1962. After a series of agonizing discussions with my grandparents, and fearing that the revolution was taking children from their parents and placing them in indoctrination camps, my parents decided to leave Cuba and everything they owned so that my younger sister and I could have a better life.

My parents had grown up in poverty and struggled to make ends meet, though by the time we left, my father had started a small welding and auto repair shop that provided for the family.

In our early years in the United States as Cuban refugees, we faced what seemed like insurmountable struggles. My experiences in American schools set

Our last family portrait in Cuba, circa 1956, showing my father Elio Angel, mother Armantina, sister Maritza, and me.

me adrift in an alien education system I could not understand. However, my parents kept a steadfast focus on education as the way to a better life for my sister and me. Though not educated themselves, my parents used every possible means to impress on us the importance of education.

My father would make his point by holding his hands up in front of me. The hands of a mechanic who has worked on engines for more than forty years have a very distinctive look. Forty years of getting burned on hot engines, cut with fan belts, soaked in grease and gasoline, and being exposed to countless harsh conditions turned my father's hands into vivid reminders that he was a man who did hard labor. He would say, "*Mira, Gera, mira a mis manos. Quiero que estudies para que cuando tú tengas mi edad tus manos no estén como las mías*—Look, Gera, look at my hands. I want you to get an education so that when you're my age your hands don't look like mine."

I did attain a college education. In fact, I became an academic and in 2000 reached the pinnacle of my academic career. I was named dean of the School of Education at Indiana University, one of America's premier educational institutions.

In May 2012, almost exactly fifty years after immigrating to the United States, I was asked by the Indiana University Alumni Association to lead a people-to-people cultural exchange tour to Cuba. In the years since my family and I had left the island, I had not thought much about a return trip. I was excited about the opportunity to go back to my native land for the first time, but I didn't know what to expect. I found the experience much more emotional than I could have imagined. And it led to a series of reflections about my life and conversations with my parents that inspired this memoir.

In Havana, automobiles from the 1950s, some in mint condition, cruised the city's streets. Until very recently, people could buy and privately operate only those cars that were on the road before the 1959 revolution. Infrastructure was neglected, leaving entire buildings crumbling and many elaborate Spanish colonial landmarks beyond restoration. Our group toured historic landmarks and United Nations Educational, Scientific and Cultural Organization (UNESCO) world heritage sites, including La Habana Vieja, the sixteenth-century city center. We also visited the Instituto Superior de Arte; the Cuban National Ballet School; a health clinic, to learn about Cuba's socialized medicine program; Ernest Hemingway's estate, Finca Vigía; and the Museo de la Revolución, which houses Cuba's most complete exhibition of its revolutionary history.

I was fascinated by everything we saw, but what I enjoyed most was talking with the local people and hearing their stories. One of my most emotional encounters happened in Trinidad, a sixteenth-century town some twenty-five miles from my Cuban hometown of Placetas. As I walked down the street with our group, an elderly man approached me with a bundle of pesos in his hands. In broken English, he said, "Mister, I change you these pesos for CUCs."

Cuba has a double economy: one that functions in pesos for the general Cuban population and one in Cuban convertible pesos (CUCs) for tourists. The average Cuban worker earns about 400 pesos per month. A CUC is roughly equal to twenty-four pesos.

Pointing to his pesos, he continued, "*Mira, mira*—Look, look—they have Che's picture on them."

I responded in Spanish, "I will trade you a CUC for your peso, but I prefer one with someone else's picture."

He promptly replied, "*Sí, sí, tengo uno con José Martí*—Yes, yes, I have one with José Martí." We had a deal. As we traded his peso for my CUC, we continued the conversation in Spanish. He said, "*Hablas español muy bien. ¿De dónde eres?*—You speak Spanish very well. Where are you from?" I told him that I was from Placetas, just a few miles from Trinidad. With a look of astonishment, he said, "From Placetas? My daughter married a boy from a medical family named Garabito and now lives in Placetas with her husband." It took me a while, then it dawned on me that Garabito had been my family physician when I lived in Cuba.

When it was time for the group to move on, the man said, "Señor, I don't blame you for not wanting a peso with Che's picture. When I was a young man, my father saved enough money to buy three small houses. His intentions were to get a little rental income from them and then, when his children grew up and married, give them the houses to live in. When the revolution came, the three houses were taken away from him." He paused and struggled to continue. "My father died of a heart attack—a broken heart, really—as a young man right after that. I'm over seventy now, and I also died the day he did."

That was one of many emotional stories I heard from local people. I was impressed by their resilience, warmth, and ability to overcome such difficult circumstances. The dual economy forces many highly educated people in Cuba to abandon their professions simply to make ends meet. An informatics professor was selling trinkets to tourists on the side of the road. He told me he could earn more in a day doing that than he could in a month working at the university. I met a nurse doing menial jobs in a cigar factory who told me the same thing. Everyone wants access to CUCs and a higher standard of living. Everyone tries to *resolver*—make do—to get by. Some people take advantage of unsuspecting tourists to make a hefty profit. Others cut corners on goods and services they produce and keep the spoils. Yet others steal products from their government employers and sell them on the black market. Pilferage is common.

Under Raúl Castro's recently enacted privatization policies, many Cubans have also been licensed to own and operate private businesses. Known as *cuentapropistas*—entrepreneurs—these business owners sell their products and services on the free market, often to tourists for CUCs, and attain a much higher standard of living than is possible on a government salary. I met an entrepreneur who had set up a sugarcane-juice stand using a traditional technique of grinding the raw cane through a small, hand-operated iron grinder. He added a shot or two of Havana Club rum, some lemon or a slice of pineapple, and sold a glass of the spiked juice to thirsty tourists for five CUCs. He was doing a brisk business.

The irony of the revolution is that it was supposed to create a classless society. Instead, it created two clear and distinct classes of people: those who have access to CUCs and those who don't. That distinction is increasing a sense of inequality as well as growing desperation and resentment over what many see as a failed promise. Most Cubans I met on the streets wanted either to leave the island or to see social and economic change. *Apagones*—Power outages—are frequent and basic conveniences unreliable. To put it bluntly, things don't work very well in Cuba. Cubans have an all-purpose catch phrase to explain the situation: "*¡Ay, es Cuba!*—Hey, it's Cuba!"

In general, my interactions with average Cubans were warm and friendly. Everyone was welcoming. When they recognized that I was Cuban, they were even more hospitable. But conversations sometimes progressed from pleasantries to issues such as poverty, housing, and jobs. Then people grew uncomfortable, perhaps for having said too much. After all, I was a perfect stranger, and for all they knew, I couldn't be trusted.

In one instance, I accompanied our tour guide to a small outdoor bar known for serving the best mojitos on the island. Mojitos are a traditional Cuban drink made with rum, lime juice, soda, mint, and sugar. It was obvious that the three bartenders took pride in making every mojito to perfection. As usual, I started talking with the workers, first about their art form, and then about life in general.

One of the bartenders was curious about what it was like for a Cuban to live in the United States. He asked me many questions about lifestyle, work, and so on. As he grew more comfortable with me, he talked about his own family. His father had left Cuba and had not been in touch for a while. Then he expressed his own unhappiness with the conditions in Cuba and spoke of his desire to leave. The other bartenders were engaged in the conversation to some extent but mostly listened. I could sense their growing discomfort about how much their colleague was disclosing to a stranger. Eventually, they pulled him away and scolded him about being careful what he said.

It seems everyone I met had an invisible line beyond which they treaded very carefully. I sometimes heard common Cubans on the streets refer to Fidel Castro as "*El Barbudo*—the Bearded One"—but in most cases, they simply did not mention either Fidel or Raúl Castro. The few references I heard tended to be warnings against mentioning their names. "*Aquí no hablamos de eso; te puede traer problemas*—Here we don't talk about that; it can bring you problems."

The fear of government expressed in these and similar conversations during my visit reminded me of stories my parents had told me about why they had decided to seek exile in the United States half a century earlier. They also resurfaced some of the fears I felt long ago as a child trying to make sense of changes I didn't understand.

## Precursors to Exile

Before the revolution, life in Placetas in the province of Las Villas (now called Villa Clara) was fairly typical of the slow pace of life in small Cuban towns. It was a peaceful and friendly community. Like most cities and towns in Cuba, Placetas had a central park that served as a community center before the revolution. The park was known as *Parque de los Laureles*—Laurel Park—because of the beautiful laurel trees that adorned its perimeter and green spaces. The park also featured a *glorieta*—band shell—in the center, iron benches, and paths where men and women walked in opposite directions to make eye contact, meet and talk, and enjoy the music. On Sundays, men wearing their fine linen *guayabera* shirts and women in their best clothes went to the Parque de los Laureles to socialize and enjoy traditional folkloric music, romantic *danzón*, and modern tunes. Men also gathered to play dominoes, smoke cigars, tell jokes, or simply recount the week's events. It was one of my father's favorite weekend and evening gathering places.

During the week, my father went to work every day as a mechanic in his *taller*—auto repair shop—and, as were most Cuban women of the time, my mother was a housewife and homemaker. We lived close to my grandparents and many aunts, uncles, and cousins. Ours was a large, close-knit family.

To understand why we upended our lives and gave up our family and friends, my father's business, and the stability of our home in Cuba, you have to understand what was happening to Cuba after Fidel Castro overthrew the dictator who preceded him, Fulgencio Batista. Batista was the president of Cuba twice: once from 1940 to 1944, then as dictator from 1952 to 1959. During his first term, he instituted a progressive constitution. At the end of that term, he moved to the United States. Many people believed in hindsight that his intention was to build up relationships with the mafia and the bosses of American gambling, drugs, and prostitution. When he returned and took over the government, he used those relationships to make the island into his personal slush fund, skimming off a percentage of all the illegal activities he'd allowed to be introduced.

Batista suspended the national constitution he'd enacted in his first term, revoked all political and union liberties, and joined with sugar barons and tobacco plantation owners to the disadvantage of the citizens. People hated his government. It was corrupt and repressive and exploited Cuba to the point where most silently prayed for his overthrow. When Fidel Castro took power, he was warmly welcomed by the vast majority of people.

My father was among the early supporters of the Castro revolution. But when it became evident that the new government was turning into just another form of repressive and autocratic dictatorship, like many other disaffected Cubans, he wanted no part of it.

Castro's changes were happening all around us. They were rapid and had an immediate impact on our lives. Chief among them was the creation in 1960 of the neighborhood Committees for the Defense of the Revolution—*Comités de Defensa de la Revolución* (or CDR)—watchdog committees with representatives in every housing block and on almost every street corner. They were to be the "eyes and ears of the revolution" and to report on "counterrevolutionary" activity on every city block (Space War 2010).

It was just like Dzerzhinsky's secret police in Russia in the 1920s. Suddenly, friends and neighbors became dangerous informants who could cause immeasurable problems for any family that didn't sympathize with the revolution. In our previously peaceful and friendly community, we felt that even the trees had eyes peering at us, and every window was like an ear, listening to what we said.

The revolution changed the ambience of the Parque de los Laureles. Loudspeakers were hung throughout the park. Instead of hearing soft music emanating from the band shell, visitors were subjected to recorded revolutionary hymns and a constant barrage of slogans praising the virtues of the revolution. As my father put it, "Everything from the loudspeakers was the revolution, the revolution, and the revolution everywhere." He continued, "You couldn't go to the park because you would get drunk on so much revolution."

During the few times my father still visited the park, he was under surveillance. On the way home one night, a neighborhood acquaintance walked past him and whispered, "You have a shadow." In other words, he was being followed. To test the warning, my father stopped suddenly as if to read a sign on one of the columns on a breezeway. He heard the "taca, tac" sound of shoes from someone following closely, but pretended he had not heard anything and continued walking. Again he stopped abruptly. Sure enough, he heard the now familiar "taca, tac." He looked back and saw a shadow dodge behind a column. My father looked around casually and continued walking.

The surveillance did not stop once my father got home. He played a small transistor radio every night before bed. He noticed that every morning a fence surrounding our house appeared to have been trampled. He decided to see whether someone was in fact walking over the fence, so each night he carefully put it back in place and went to bed, listening to his radio. In the morning, the fence had clearly been trampled. As he put it, "*De noche pasaban por la cerca para ver lo que yo oía*—At night they would go over the fence to see what I was listening to. They wanted to know if it was some form of counterrevolutionary communication." With a laugh, he said he never listened to counterrevolutionary stations—only music. *"Música, música y cuando se apagaban las luces me acostaba a dormir*—Music, music and when the lights went out, I just went to sleep."

*"Pero todas las mañanas la cerca estaba achatada, constantemente*—But every morning the fence was trampled, constantly."

My parents were not considered counterrevolutionaries, which in those days would have gotten them executed by firing squad. But Cuban authorities knew they did not sympathize with the revolution.

## Postrevolution Turmoil

In the early days of the revolution, my father received notice of a meeting for regional business owners in Santa Clara, the capital of Las Villas province. The discussion topic was forming a cooperative and bringing all the privately owned businesses into a single operation to be managed by the owners under government auspices. He did not want to go but felt compelled to see what was happening. A well-spoken government official took charge of the meeting and said that those present comprised the official assembly that would advise on how to unite all the small businesses into a major cooperative. Attendees had to take turns speaking on the matter. When my father's turn came, he said, "Well, I'd like to know if what you're proposing is voluntary or obligatory."

"Comrade, it's voluntary," said the official in charge. My father remembers the entire assembly quieting down after his question.

"Well, if this is voluntary, my business is not yours. But if it is obligatory, the business is yours as of this moment," my father said. "But my preference is that it not be that way."

The very next day, my father was completely cut off from suppliers and other vendors he needed to conduct his business. He could no longer function, even though his business was a small shop with just a few tools. He couldn't even get the metal bars needed for welding. "And thereafter the neighborhood committee was constantly watching."

Although I was only eight at the time of the Castro takeover, I remember the turmoil within my family and in society following the revolution. My parents didn't talk much about the revolution or their feelings about it, but I knew they feared the government would break up the family and send my sister and me to indoctrination camps in the countryside. It took only a year and a half of living with that fear for my parents to decide Cuba was no longer for them. If my sister and I were to live as normal and happy children, the family had to get out. My parents decided to request permission from the Cuban government to let us go to the United States. They downplayed the decision, however, telling my sister and me that we were going to visit our uncle *"en el Gran Norte*—in the Great North," as my mother called the United States.

My uncle had moved there years before the revolution. We admired him for taking that step on his own and establishing himself in the United States, which my parents considered the best country in the world. When the Cuban revolution began to turn sour in my parents' mouths, I remember my mother saying to me, "We'll soon be visiting your uncle. Isn't that wonderful?"

And for me, it was, because it soon became known on the streets of Placetas that my whole family was going to leave Cuba to live in the United States. I was singled out on the streets, in shops, and on playgrounds because the revolution-aries saw our family as rejecting the revolution and scurrying off the island on our bellies, like cowards. They called us *gusanos*—worms.

To make it worse, I was an overweight schoolboy in a Catholic school. Catholicism, churches, and religious schools were seen as enemies of the State, to be dealt with at some future time for being antirevolutionary. I grew afraid about what was happening all around me. Even though it meant leaving my friends, I secretly began to look forward to leaving Cuba and starting a new life. People with highly specialized skills (such as doctors, engineers, and other professionals) were not allowed to leave because their skills were too valuable for the revolution. But my father was a simple car mechanic, so we were expendable. Castro was happy to get rid of people like my mother and father, who didn't support the revolution.

## The Telegram

Leaving wasn't that simple, however. On February 7, 1962, my parents received a telegram addressed to my younger sister, Maritza Justa González Torres, then five years old, directing her to report to Havana on February 9 for departure to the United States. My parents went into a panic. Months earlier, they had requested permission from the Cuban government for our family of four to emigrate.

My father, Elio Angel González, immediately began to explore the possibil-ity of sending my sister to the United States alone, hoping the rest of the family would be able to follow her later. He contacted the Catholic Church. At the time, it ran the underground program that became known as *Operación Pedro Pan*—Operation Peter Pan, which took unaccompanied Cuban children to the United States and placed them with temporary caretakers until their parents could join them (Pedropan.org, n.d.). He also contacted my uncle, Manuel González, who was living in Miami and could look after my sister until the rest of us could join her. But my mother, Armantina González Torres, would not let either of her children go unless the entire family could leave together. To this day, she recalls saying, "*O nos vamos todos juntos, o no se va ninguno*—We all go together or none of us leaves."

Much to their relief, later that day, my parents received another state tele-gram from the Cuban Ministry of Communications, granting permission for all four of us to leave. We were instructed to report to Havana at least seventy-two

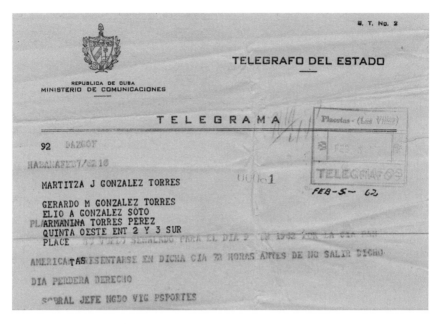

State telegram giving my family instructions on the date and time of our departure from Cuba.

hours before our scheduled departure via Pan Am airlines on February 9. The telegram was dated February 5, but local authorities had held onto it for two days.

As usual, that day I rode home from school on my bike. My mother greeted me outside excitedly, saying, *"Gera, apúrate, apúrate el telegrama llegó. Solo tenemos unas horas para arreglarnos—*Hurry, hurry, the telegram has arrived. We only have a few hours to get ready." The confusion that surrounded the telegram's arrival and events during our last days in Cuba was characteristic of the turmoil in the country, in my hometown, and in the province of Las Villas during the months and years immediately following Castro's defeat of the Batista regime. My parents feared for the family.

When I returned to the island in 2012, it was evident that many of the people with whom I spoke, like the bartenders serving mojitos, still feared those in power and knew what could happen to them for stepping out of line. Moved by the stories I heard, I asked my parents to tell me more about why they left. Without hesitation, my mother said, *"Porque se veía lo que venía—*Because we could see what was coming." She said that the first thing the revolution did was nationalize private schools, and that San Antonio, my elementary school, was one of the first to be nationalized in Placetas. She and my father refused to live in

Sitting at a school desk in Colegio San Antonio, my Catholic school in Placetas, circa 1959.

a country where the government would take control of the children: "*¡Ay, ni, ni, ni, no!*—Ay, never, never, never, no!"

My father had a slightly more complicated answer. He said the government started to change the system right away. He asked me if I knew what *Patria Protestad* was. I didn't. I learned it refers to an ancient Roman doctrine that granted the father and the mother and, in their absence, the grandparents, legal custody and power over their children, whom they had a duty to protect. In 1960, rumors started circulating in Cuba that the government of Fidel Castro intended to abolish parental rights based on Patria Protestad and take children between the ages of six and sixteen from their parents and send them to indoctrination camps in the Soviet Union and remote parts of Cuba. There's controversy about how the Patria Protestad rumors started. Some people claim it was part of a CIA-inspired plot to play traditionally strong family bonds against the revolution. Others say they were based on efforts by the Castro government to break family bonds to benefit the revolution. Whatever the case, my father believed that one day the government would come in, declare that Maritza and I were "*hijos de la revolución*—children of the revolution," and take us away from him and our mother. He said, "*Entonces nosotros le cogimos miedo a eso*—We were frightened by that."

## A Difficult Decision

Mindful of the impact leaving the country would have on my grandparents and the rest of the family, when the time came to decide, my father gathered his mother, Encarnación de la Cruz Soto; his mother's sister, our great-aunt Luisa, who was very close to us; and his father, Manuel (Manolo) González Méndez, for a family discussion. If they agreed we should leave, he and my mother would immediately begin preparations. But, he said, "*Si ustedes no están de acuerdo, aquí nos quedamos todos y cada uno sabe que no puede salir*—If you do not agree, we will stay and everyone in the family will know that we cannot leave." My grandparents and Luisa put our interests first, saying, "*Nosotros somos viejos. ¡Vete y llévate los muchachos! ¡Vete!*—We are old. Go and take the children! Go!"

During our conversations decades later, I asked my parents what was the most difficult thing about leaving.

"Look, everything was difficult," my father said. "Everything was difficult, and it broke my heart. I cried." But he knew that he needed to be strong in front of the family. What made it so painful was that Manolo, Encarnación, and Luisa had essentially raised Maritza and me. Even though we slept at home at night, he said it was our grandparents and Luisa who had looked after us to make sure we went to school and that all our needs were met. He had to go to work and my mother had to take care of the home, he said, but my grandparents and Luisa were always there for us.

"When the moment came that I had to rip you away from Manolo, that was terrible for me," my father admitted. But it was even more painful knowing that he was taking us away from my grandmother and Luisa. He was an emotional wreck. "Luisa did not have children, no, but you were her children. And Encarnación—to this day I still can't even talk about it." He continued, "They were supporting me to go forward, to take you out of there."

He admitted that if his father, Manolo, had started to cry in front of him he wouldn't have been able to stand it. "Since everyone supported us, everything turned out well, of course," he said. "But they were left completely empty."

My mother's father was equally supportive. My maternal grandmother, Elvira, died when my mother was just three years old, and my grandfather, Adriano, remained the head of a large household of eight sisters and brothers. He didn't remarry until late in life because he didn't want a stepmother raising his children. Well aware of what our leaving meant to him, my mother said, "I don't remember the right proverb, but my father used to say that the family always had to be together."

# 2  The Great North

Once my parents requested permission to leave Cuba, the government took inventory of everything we owned. We were allowed to use our belongings until our departure but could not sell or give away anything. That's the way the system worked. You applied for an exit permit, the government took stock of everything you owned, then you waited until you were notified whether permission was granted. The state telegram was the final, official step telling you when you could leave.

The day the telegram arrived I awoke at night to strange noises in our house. Under cover of darkness, my father and his friends were moving a mattress from our house to my grandmother's. Our mattress was better than hers, but it had been inventoried. My father and his friends had to be vigilant and move when the neighborhood committee's guards were distracted or not expecting it. "Those CDR committees could report you for doing something like switching a mattress," my father said.

My father had had a previous brush with the CDR when he sold a piece of furniture to a friend and the committee made him bring it back. Ironically, an army colonel took an interest in the piece and told my father he wanted to buy it. My father explained that he couldn't sell it, but the colonel assured him it would be fine. He later loaded the furniture on the back of a truck while the CDR looked the other way. However, switching my grandmother's mattress was another matter.

The switch went undetected. Early the next day, we headed for Havana, accompanied by my grandmother Encarnación and Conrado (Lalo) Hernandez, my father's best friend. Lalo drove us in a 1952 Ford my father used to fix for him and sometimes borrowed. I don't remember much about that trip except that it was quiet. I must have been watching the royal palms along the Cuban countryside pass by as I had done many times before on family road trips. I had no idea it would be decades before I again laid eyes on such a mesmerizing sight.

Neither did I know that leaving would so profoundly affect our lives. Nor did I realize how education would justify my parents' sacrifices. All I could think of was that we were finally on our way to the Great North.

## At the Airport

In Havana, another childhood friend of my father's, Luis García, put us up in his apartment. As my father tells the story, "In those days, anyone would help anyone else out. We just threw a couple of mattresses on the floor and spent the night there."

After a sleepless night, we headed for the airport. My father carried a few pieces of jewelry—a gold chain, a religious medal, and a gold ring—and an old silver peso that a friend had given him for good luck. He had also hidden a few dollar bills inside the soles of his shoes because he knew the government would not let us take any money. But at the airport, everyone was searched, so he decided to leave everything except the silver peso. If found, he reasoned that he'd try to explain it was a good luck charm and, if necessary, just leave it behind too. He gave the shoes to Lalo and the jewelry to my grandmother. He also told my mother not to try to take anything.

But my mother did not listen. Instead, she hid her engagement ring and two small gold chains, one belonging to my sister and one to me, among the clothes in her suitcase. She was terrified that the officials would find the jewelry, but she didn't want to part with it. Those pieces were too meaningful.

As expected, once we had said our goodbyes to the family and friends who had accompanied us and proceeded to security, my father and my mother were subjected to intensive searches. Fortunately, the officials did not find the jewelry my mother had hidden or the silver dollar my father was carrying. Still, my father also faced a series of false accusations.

"An official told me I couldn't leave because I was a medical doctor," my father remembered. "I had been working as a mechanic right up to the day we left, so I showed him my hands, which were full of grease, and asked him if they looked like doctor's hands. He left the interrogation room and then came back and said we could leave, but first I'd have to pay $200 for a telephone bill we had left unpaid. I told him that was not possible, because we didn't have a telephone. He banged on the desk and disappeared into the back office. When he came back, he said that it was a mistake, but we definitely had to leave the keys to the car. I told him we didn't have a car, either."

"But they kept looking for excuses to make things difficult," my father continued. "Just before the telegram arrived, I had cut a tendon in my finger and had fashioned a sling from metal scraps in my shop to help support and protect the injured finger. The official asked me what the sling was and I told him. Then he claimed the sling was an orthopedic medical device and I had to leave it. So I had to take it off. Ironically, they didn't say anything about the two bottles of rum I had purchased at the airport." Cuban rum, made famous by the Bacardí brand, was coveted in the United States, and the Cuban government wanted to create an international market for what was known as one of the best rums in the world. The government was already struggling economically and needed cash. Since Cuban rum was a source of hard currency, the airport officials were glad to let it go through.

At a final baggage inspection, a government official slashed my father's duffle bag, causing its contents to spill to the floor. With our hearts pounding, my father and I scrambled to collect our belongings as the airplane sat at the gate with its engines running.

Even after we boarded the plane, the ordeal continued. Just before takeoff, a Jeep pulled up, carrying a colonel and an armed guard. They boarded the plane and walked up and down the aisle. Everyone was silent. My parents were shaking. To everyone's relief, the colonel said, "*Vamos, los esbirros no están aquí*—Let's go, the *esbirros* are not here." *Esbirros*, the Spanish word for henchmen, was used by the Castro government for Cubans who had served as officials of the Batista regime.

Once the plane took off, everyone remained quiet. When the pilot announced, "We have left Cuban airspace. We will be landing in Miami in forty-five minutes," the entire cabin broke into celebratory screaming and applause. Years later, my mother recalled, "*Cuando oí esas palabras se me cayó el alma*—When I heard those words my soul dropped."

I knew when I heard those words that my life would change forever. I was anxious and fearful. But I kept hearing my mother's and father's words about going to the Great North. Somehow they made me feel everything would be all right.

## Refugees in Miami

As the plane prepared to land, my legal status wasn't on my mind. I was thinking about the people I'd left behind and the life I would lead in my new adopted nation of the United States of America. When my family left Cuba, we had been granted a visa waiver by the US authorities that enabled us to enter the country as exiles, to be processed by the Cuban Refugee Center. I wouldn't understand my legal status as a refugee and an immigrant till much later.

A bright-red sign came on in the DC3 plane that read "No Smoking," and I remember feeling so proud that I could read a word of English. I was entering a new world with a new language, and I was really excited about getting there. I still feared what had happened at the airport and the confusion and danger. I thought of my grandparents, my aunt, and Hugo Morales, my best friend, who lived right next door to my grandmother's house and with whom I had spent many hours on family trips and at play. Would I ever see him again? He was the one friend I would miss. But I felt safe being with my family.

On Friday, February 9, 1962, nine months before the Cuban missile crisis, we arrived in Miami. We carried one suitcase and the two bottles of Cuban rum my father had purchased at the airport in Havana.

I looked at my father and mother and saw that they were anxious. Was this real? Did they have the right papers? Did they need anything more for immigration and getting through US customs?

Reassured by my mother's words that life in the Great North would be wonderful, I dismissed their anxiety as the effects of what we had just been through at the airport in Cuba. But I was wrong. Even in Miami, the interrogation ordeal continued. My father was separated from the rest of the family and questioned

My paternal grandfather's birthday celebration. My grandparents Manolo and Encarnación are standing in the center. My best friend Hugo Morales (*top right with bottle*) and I (*behind grandfather's shoulder*) looked forward to these happy annual celebrations.

by customs officials because they thought he might be a communist sympathizer. Apparently, the FBI had an Elio González on its list of Communist Party members.

Years earlier, in 1956, my father had spent a year in the United States on a work visa. He'd lived in New York City. The officials asked for details of that year and pulled out a file with photos of him in Manhattan. My father recalled the conversation about one particularly memorable photo. "I was walking past the corner of Eighty-Sixth Street near Central Park, which was close to where I used to live, heading for the subway with my lunch box. The customs official asked, 'Is this you?' And I said, 'Yes.' After a few more questions, they talked among themselves and told me everything I said had been corroborated. They apologized and said I was not the Elio González they were looking for. It was okay to proceed through immigration."

Getting through immigration took us a lot longer than most of the other people who had arrived on our flight but, several hours later, we were finally done. After we were processed, we boarded a bus and were taken to the Tamiami Hotel, where Cuban refugees were housed until they could be documented and claimed by other family members or sponsors. The Tamiami was an old hotel in the heart of downtown Miami, right on the corner of West Flagler Street and Second Avenue, a short walking distance from the Centro Hispano Católico, which served as the offices for the Cuban Refugee Center. The Tamiami had opened its doors in 1920 as a six-floor, one-hundred-room, chic European-style hotel. It was advertised as the most perfectly ventilated hotel in the South, where "a cheerful welcome awaits you." (Florida Memory, n.d.)

As we entered the hotel, however, I was struck by how dark and musty the lobby was. Clearly, the years of hot, humid South Florida weather and rapid development all around the hotel had taken their toll. There was no ventilation. A doorman dressed in black pants and a white short-sleeved shirt greeted us. Noticing the two bottles of Cuban rum my father was holding, he asked whether he wanted to sell them. Without hesitation, my father said, "*Sí*—Yes," and sold them to the doorman for five dollars. That put a big smile on the doorman's face, who, as advertised, cheerfully waved us in.

My father later learned that those bottles of rum were worth a lot more in the United States, but he didn't care because we were so desperate for money.

The next day, we registered with the Cuban Refugee Center. Lines at the center snaked around the block. As we waited to be documented, a lady behind me took a special interest in me. She wanted to know where we were from, how old I was, what school I had attended in Cuba, what grade I was in, when we had arrived, and other details about our travels. I suppose she felt sorry for us, because when it was our turn to move on, she pulled out a dollar and gave it to me, "*Para que compres Chiclets*—So you can buy some Chiclets gum," she said. My father watched this transaction. When we were safely out of her sight, he said to me, "*Gera, déjame guardar el dólar para que no se te pierda*—Gera, let me hold the dollar so you don't lose it." I never saw that dollar again. Our financial circumstances were so dire at the time that a dollar must have seemed like a lot of money.

After we were officially registered as Cuban refugees, my father's brother Manuel picked us up and took us to the home of his mother-in-law. It was a small duplex she shared with my uncle's family and her son's family. We stayed there for a few days until the first government assistance check arrived. As refugees, we were eligible to receive eighty dollars a month for three months. With that check and a little borrowed cash, we rented a small efficiency apartment. The borrowed money also allowed my father to buy a few tools in the hope of finding work among friends and acquaintances in the South Florida Cuban community.

"I knew a little English from my stay in New York, but I wanted to make contacts, learn more English, and be able to work. That was my first priority," my father recalled. "To us, this country was the greatest thing on earth and the best place we could possibly be."

## A New Beginning

Our new home was a tiny apartment with a small kitchen and living room, one bathroom, and a closet-sized bedroom my parents shared with my sister and me. Our sole source of entertainment was a small black-and-white RCA television, a

My parents in the living room of our first apartment in Miami. The black-and-white RCA TV
was our only source of entertainment.

gift from my uncle's brother-in-law. The apartment sat on the edge of the area that
became known as Little Havana. The sobriquet "Little Havana" was applied to the
Shenandoah and Riverside neighborhoods, a sprawling area west of Downtown
Miami where, attracted by low rents, the concentration of Cubans grew sharply following the vast influx of Cuban refugees in the 1960s (World Heritage Encyclopedia,
n.d.). During that period, there were three flights a day from Havana to Miami,
each one full of refugees.

In those days, Miami was not the international center of banking and Latin
American commerce it is today. Instead, it was a sleepy little retirement town, and
work was hard to come by, especially for immigrants. Using the tools acquired
with borrowed money, my father started working on commission as a mechanic

at a Sunoco gas station on the corner of Calle Ocho (Eighth Street) and SW Nineteenth Avenue, the heart of Little Havana. It was within walking distance of our apartment, convenient for someone without transportation. Work was slow and income quite limited. As my father recalled, there was a funeral home across the street from the gas station, and from time to time they would call on him to come help "*mover al muerto*—move the deceased." It was a small but important source of additional income.

My father also managed to buy a broken-down 1948 Plymouth for thirty dollars. It had a blown engine. He worked on it slowly to get it in running condition. As soon as he was able to use it, he put his few tools in the trunk and started doing small auto repair jobs for friends at their houses on weekends and at night, adding to the commission he made at the gas station.

Try as she might, my mother could not find work. My father had to take a second job working the night shift at a sugar mill on the edge of the Everglades, north of Miami. That did not last long, though. He recalls having to drive for miles after dark on small, winding roads with trucks full of sugarcane coming from the other direction. It was too dangerous.

## Buena Conducta

Aside from the economic hardship, that initial year in Miami was personally difficult for me for another reason: it was my first experience of an American school. I was one of thousands of non-English-speaking Cuban and other Hispanic students who had moved into the Miami-Dade County Public Schools system. I was bewildered by the large number of adults in the school, from principals to teachers to custodians, with seemingly unconnected roles, trying to cope with the large number of Spanish-speaking kids who, like me, were lost and overwhelmed. Some of us were placed in what were called immersion programs. This was the sink-or-swim approach to cultural assimilation, and learning English through direct exposure to the language and interaction with American kids. Others were placed in transitional programs where they learned English in stages in special language classes, then moved into regular classrooms. And some ended up in bilingual programs where all the Spanish-speaking kids were placed in separate special classes taught mostly in Spanish.

I attended Shenandoah Middle School, an old Mediterranean-style, multi-floor facility with a big arched entrance that served my Little Havana neighborhood. I was originally placed in an immersion program, but when it became clear I was struggling, I was moved to a bilingual education classroom. What happened to me in that classroom had a profound impact on my education for years to come. I can see now from my perspective as an educator that the school administrators didn't understand that the new Cuban students faced more than a language problem. We also faced a cultural adjustment problem. Most of us still wore the clothes we brought from Cuba or hand-me-downs from charitable organizations or the refugee center. We were loud and spoke with our hands. We even had trouble sitting in the neat rows of desks that awaited us each morning. Some spoke better English than others and tried to help those who, like me, struggled with the language. But we were all lost in an institution with rules we didn't understand. We were going through the turmoil of adjusting to a new life while trying to adapt and fit in. We were behaving the best way we knew how, but it didn't take long for us to become known as the troublemakers.

In today's language of education, we wouldn't have been described as "troublemakers," but as good-natured kids—a bit rowdy, but happy and lively. In those more authoritarian, teacher-centered days, we were a mob of kids who had to be controlled and forced to submit to the authority of the school. So the school sent in the vice principal in charge of discipline to set us straight.

He was a tall man with a crew cut who looked as if he'd recently retired from the armed services. He wore straight-legged khaki pants and a plaid button-down, collared shirt. He was straight-backed, authoritarian in his walk and manner, and unwavering in his determination to have the school run like the Navy—shipshape and precise. And he wouldn't tolerate any bad behavior, disrespect for authority, or abuse of school processes. He was intimidating. And he was determined to make an example of us so that his lesson would run like a horror story through our ranks.

His entry into our classroom was presaged by our bilingual teacher telling us, "You'd all better be on your best behavior, because the vice principal is on his way to our class."

It was like announcing the arrival of the archangel Gabriel, here to mete out judgment. When the classroom door opened, in walked a figure I'd seen only from a distance. He was literally larger than life. He stood at the front of the class and rocked back and forth on his feet, viewing us with his narrowed eyes, assaying us as if to determine how severe to make his punishment.

Suddenly, he banged the desk with his massive fist. We jumped. He shouted at us, "You all here are behaving disgracefully. Your behavior has brought shame to the school, and it will not be tolerated. You have come to this country of Americans, and that's what I'm going to make you, an American, whether you like it or not!"

It went on like this for some time. But it all went over my head. I was so scared I hardly understood a word he was saying. And so, in all innocence, I turned to my friend, José, who spoke better English, and asked him, "*¿José, que dice ese hombre?*—José, what's that man saying?"

The vice principal looked directly at me for daring to interrupt him. He marched to the back of the class, grabbed me by the arm, and dragged me out of my desk to the front of the class. In broken Spanish, he barked, "*¡Buena conducta!*

*¡Buena conducta!*—Good conduct! Good conduct!—Act properly!" I barely understood as he yelled, "This is America and you better behave like Americans or you will all be thrown out of school!"

I was red-faced and humiliated. Everybody was looking at me. They were expressionless, afraid of smiling or smirking. The vice principal looked at the class with cold dispassion, almost contempt. Nobody breathed. Nobody spoke or made a sound. We were terrified.

After scaring the class to death, which obviously was his aim, he dragged me by the arm and toward the classroom door. Our bilingual teacher turned to the other students as they sat, astonished and horrified by the vice principal's treatment. She said, "*Compórtensen bien porque esto le puede pasar a ustedes*—Behave well because this can happen to you." Then she turned to the vice principal and, looking at me, softly said something to him in English I could not understand.

I sensed she was standing up for me but I was too humiliated to comprehend what was happening. Possibly because the teacher had just spoken to students in Spanish in front of him, the vice principal became even more irritated, ignored her and pulled me out the door. I was summarily suspended from school just because I'd asked José the question, "What's that man saying?"

The school called my mother. I had been suspended and she needed to come pick me up. My mother didn't understand, so she told the school to call my father at work. He was furious. My father was a small, quiet man, but he had a big temper, perhaps something he inherited from my grandmother Encarnación, a strict disciplinarian. From my father's perspective, I was misbehaving and putting at risk my future and all that he and my mother had sacrificed. Although my parents were not educated, they knew education was the key to their children's success. My father often reminded me by showing me his hands and imploring me to get an education so my hands wouldn't look like those of a mechanic. Yet, here I was, suspended from school.

My father was from the old country, where respect for authority and discipline were not only expected, but strictly enforced. At the gas station, he had cut out a rubber belt from one of the old tires. When he got home, much earlier than usual that evening, he immediately went into a fury. My mother recalled, "He gave you a terrible beating." She said our neighbor in the apartment next door had to intervene. My mother said, "*Tu padre fue un bruto*—Your father was a brute."

The next day my father took me to the school and asked to speak with my teacher. We waited nervously in the front office. He asked my teacher for forgiveness and asked to speak with the school principal. My teacher said that was impossible, but my father said he wouldn't leave until he had. Soon the principal appeared—a tall man, my father recalled—and asked, "How can I help you?" My father explained in broken English that he understood I had been suspended for misbehaving at school. Then he asked for an interpreter and said, "The only thing

My parents and sister waiting for me after school.

I've come to ask is that you give me another opportunity, just one. I don't want two, only one—that you take my son back." The principal told my father to go in peace. I would be allowed to return to school the next day.

And so I did. But I had learned a very important lesson: to keep my mouth shut. From that day on, I never participated in class activities, never raised my hand to ask a question, never initiated a class discussion, and never in any other way engaged in the learning process. I didn't make trouble. I wasn't a truant. I just sat in class and quietly let time go by. Pretty soon, the system forgot about me. I became invisible. Some moments in a child's life pass by unnoticed; others affect the entire life. I was a child who just wanted to fit in. But the way I was treated was so shocking and humiliating that it influenced my behavior over the next several years. It also made me determined, as a future educator of thousands of young men and women, to change the way kids were treated in schools.

Reminiscing on that school experience years later, my father told me, "I don't recall, but I don't think you had any more problems there." For sure, none he ever heard about!

## Plan B

After a year of trying to find steady work and make ends meet, my parents decided that the economic situation in Miami was so dire that they would have to relocate. The US government, realizing that the South Florida economy could not absorb the large number of Cuban refugees who arrived daily, had created a program that became known as the Cuban Refugee Relocation Service. It provided travel assistance for Cubans who wanted to leave Florida and resettle in another part of the United States. To help them get started, it provided travel support and put them in touch with charity groups and others who could provide assistance in their new communities.

Frustrated by the lack of productive work opportunities, my father told the Cuban Refugee Relocation Service that he wanted to relocate his family. My father didn't care where they sent us as long as he could find work and use his skills as a mechanic, welder, and machinist—a place "where there's industry," my father said. My father's entire life had been one of "purification of the soul" through hard work: "*El trabajo purifica el alma*—Work purifies the soul," he used to say. Work, work, work. When things didn't turn out as expected, he picked himself up and started all over again. He never complained, never blamed anyone else—except, perhaps, Fidel Castro—for the life of work he lived and the hard lessons he learned. All he wanted was to work and support his family. The Relocation Service attendant looked in a book of approved destinations for a place labeled as an industrial city. He put his finger on a line and said to my father, "Here it is—Pittsburgh."

As an adult looking back, leaving Florida was the same as leaving Cuba. When we left our home island, I was relieved that when I arrived in the Great North, the traumas of social rejection and bullying would end.

In Florida, I experienced the same life I'd suffered in Cuba. I was punished for no crime or offense, but for who I was: a lively, excited, and enthusiastic kid who wanted to settle in but simply didn't know how to conform. In my cultural immersion classes, the American kids made fun of me because I didn't understand the culture or the language. And when I was transferred to the bilingual class, I was humiliated, then suspended by a vice principal who wanted to make an example out of me. It felt as though I'd not progressed at all from the nightmares of my Cuban life.

The decision to move to Pittsburgh came as an enormous relief. I was going to a new place, a new beginning, and a new hope.

Perhaps in Pittsburgh, life would be better. Perhaps …

# 3 Into the Cold

My father told me how exciting it would be to live in a city covered in winter snow. I trusted my father's judgment; after all, he'd lived in New York. Leaving the sun and warmth of Florida would be the beginning of a new adventure and a better life. He described the new food we'd be eating, the wonderful customs, the opportunities, and even the exciting places where we'd live.

I tried to show enthusiasm. But I had no concept of where I was going. It was yet another move, another relocation, and more disruption and uncertainty.

Armed with winter coats donated by Catholic Charities, we prepared for the cold. I didn't like the fact that my coat was a green woman's coat. Later my mother recalled, "You didn't want to wear the coat because it was a woman's coat, don't you remember?" Coat or no coat, I tried to believe that life could get better.

On February 7, 1963, almost a year to the day we arrived in Miami, I again found myself in a DC3 plane. When we landed at Pittsburgh International Airport, the flight attendant said over the loudspeaker, "Welcome to Pittsburgh. Please remember to put on your coats. The temperature outside is five below zero." I had no concept of "below zero." When the plane stopped its engines, the disembarkation ladder was attached, and the plane doors opened, I found out.

I had never experienced anything like it. My father had described the excitement of snow and the games I could play. But when the frozen North hit my body, I shook with cold. What kind of place was this? I quickly pulled on the green woman's coat. When we got off the plane, my ears froze. This was an entirely new kind of pain. "You'll get used to it," my father said. I had no choice.

My mother reminded us to make sure the blue-white-and-yellow buttons from the Cuban Refugee Relocation Service in Miami were clearly visible on our coat lapels. The buttons read: "Catholic Relief Services—N.C.W.C." In the middle stood a big cross. They were the means by which the Catholic Charities volunteers would identify us at the airport. Sure enough, Mr. Sebastian immediately recognized us. "*Un viejito muy bueno*—A very nice old man," my mother recalled years later. Mr. Sebastian welcomed us to Pittsburgh and said he was glad that we had arrived safely. He said there was another Cuban family in the area, but they lived fifty miles away.

The first order of business was to get us settled into our new living quarters in government-subsidized housing arranged by Catholic Charities. We had a small row-house apartment in the borough of McKees Rocks, just outside Pittsburgh.

My sister and I walking home from school in our first Pittsburgh snowfall.

The apartment complex sat atop a hill that overlooked the Ohio River and the metropolis of Pittsburgh. A steep wooden staircase hugged the sides of the hill and led to shopping areas and public transportation routes below. Residents could walk down those long steps to the shopping areas, but it was not easy. On cold winter days, the steps were very wet and slippery. If it snowed, they were impossible to navigate. At least, that was the case for me—I'd never lived in a place where it snowed.

In its heyday, McKees Rocks was a steel-producing union town with large railroad machine shops and manufacturers of locomotives and freight and passenger cars. You could look over the Ohio River to Pittsburgh and see reaching into the sky the huge stacks of some of the largest steel mills in the country.

But by the time we arrived in McKees Rocks, all the manufacturing plants were shut down, as were the steel mills in Pittsburgh. "There were gigantic plants. They were a grand spectacle, many square blocks in size, but they were all shut down," my father recalls. The place seemed like a dirty, dilapidated ghost town.

The saddest and most unsettling aspect of that time was the way everything around me kept devolving. Again and again, just as I started to develop roots, just as I began to feel the ground beneath my feet turn solid and permanent, I found myself on the edge of quicksand.

My memories of those days remain vivid. Today, as a husband and a father, I remember being a little boy of twelve, living in a desperately impoverished part of the United States, cramped together as a family in a run-down, two-bedroom row house. I think of my mother and father, deprived of privacy, lying in bed and whispering to each other. My sister and I could hear every word, and we knew that their language was of fear for our family's welfare. Sometimes in the other room we pretended to read and play, all the while glancing into our parents' bedroom. Again, their whispers and looks of concern said we were in dire straits.

I remember my quiet and gentle father, who only occasionally gave way to anger and frustration, reading the newspaper advertisements day after disheartening day, trying to find an employer who would give him work. He wanted to get back to the work he loved as a welder and mechanic, repairing broken engines. But he would have taken any job if it meant putting dollars in his pocket to support his family and returning each night with a feeling of self-respect. I remember the look on my beloved mother's face, the desperation in her eyes, the way she tried to comfort my father and assure him that tomorrow, or the next day, their fortune would change, and the Great North Land of America would provide him with the dignity of work. But when my father closed the newspaper in anger and resentment and said that today, just as yesterday and the day before, there was no work, my mother couldn't hide her own sadness and despair.

Try as he might, my father never found work in Pittsburgh. There were no jobs. Hope turned into despondency. We had food and shelter, but that didn't make our lives easy. We had no car and we had to walk everywhere, even for life's simplest necessities.

The cold was especially hard on my mother. I remember her slipping on the streets and crying in pain from the cold, the ice, and the frustration of not being able to lead her once-familiar simple life. Whenever she went outside, her face and hands turned white from the cold. We created a routine to warm her when she came back, sometimes rushing to get a pan of warm water to heat her arms and legs to restore her circulation. But over time, instead of encouraging us and assuring us that tomorrow things would be better, she'd burst into tears from the frustration and pain of her frozen hands and feet. All my young life, my mother

My parents and sister bundled up in the Pittsburgh winter.

had been my bedrock. Now I watched her grow frail and dependent. This terrified me.

My father's approach to the freezing cold was different, possibly because he'd spent a year in New York and was more used to it, or because he was physically stronger than my mother. He'd put on his Russian-style cap with earflaps lined with fur and go out to face the elements. His main concern was not being able to find work. He tried to keep our spirits up, talking about the fun trips we could take, when we had enough money, to enjoy the beauty of the changing seasons in the North.

His enthusiasm just might have worked, had it not been for the reality of my mother's tears.

The problem was more than the alienation we felt in the ice and snow of the industrial North. It was also the intense loneliness. I had no friends—no interactions with anybody. Without a car in difficult weather, life for us was lonely and isolated and we longed for friendships and relationships.

## A Hail Mary Pass

My sister and I were enrolled at Holy Trinity Catholic School on free tuition scholarships, but there was no school bus service. Word had gotten around that a Cuban family had moved into the neighborhood. Parents and kids alike were curious. They wanted to see what Cubans looked like. Every day when my sister and I left our row-house apartment to walk to school, a crowd of kids waited for us outside, like a lynch mob in some B-grade Western movie. They surrounded us and pointed at us as if we were exhibits in a zoo and ridiculed us. And they followed us, the new kids from the project, because we were some sort of curiosity.

It was humiliating, and I was intimidated and frightened. I couldn't comprehend their words or their ridicule. But I can only imagine that they were amazed to see that Cubans didn't wear loincloths or drink from coconuts. My sister must have been a special curiosity because she had very light skin, blonde hair, and blue eyes. The constant laughing and teasing was unbearable. My sister and I didn't leave our apartment unless it was absolutely necessary. My sister cried every day when it was time to go to school. She didn't want to go because she was afraid and, besides, she couldn't understand the nuns.

My suspension at Shenandoah was still fresh in my mind: I didn't want to cause any trouble. This wasn't my first Catholic school experience. In Cuba, I had attended first through fifth grade at El Colegio San Antonio, a Jesuit school in Placetas. Although Holy Trinity was different, in a strange sort of way, I found solace in the school. When we arrived in the morning, to avoid contact with other students and teachers, I went directly to the school chapel. During recess and lunch and any other moment I wasn't required to be in class, I went to the chapel. After school, while I waited for my sister or sometimes my parents for the long, cold walk home, again I went to the chapel.

I am a Catholic, but not extreme in my faith. Yet the church and school chapel directed my heart and mind to inner contemplation. And that's what I so badly needed. I needed a refuge, a place where I could withdraw from school and family, from Pittsburgh and the depressed industrial North, from my life as an exile who was bullied and threatened and harassed. I needed an environment where I wasn't the subject of finger-pointing boys and girls determined to exclude me and teach me a lesson for the sin of being a Cuban refugee. I needed a place where bullying teachers couldn't find me, haul me in front of the class, and ridicule me.

I didn't speak the language of those around me, so I was excluded from everything. I had nobody to talk to. Whenever I said something, I feared the ridicule of my classmates, the nuns, and the priests. There was no reason to fear the nuns—they were kindness itself and helpful. But because of my experiences in Miami, I had an overwhelming fear of rejection and abuse. The chapel was a place for solipsism, for inner thoughts. It was the one place where I didn't have to interact with anybody, where I could be alone with my thoughts and God, who perhaps, just perhaps could explain my situation to me, and help me out of the misery my life had become.

The sisters who ran the school noticed how much time I was spending in the chapel. What they took to be my religious devotion and prayer must have endeared me to them, because at the end of the semester, my parents received a simple mimeographed sheet that read:

> "Dear Parent,
>
> Your child has been promoted to Grade 7.
>
> Sister Catherine Hoberta, Principal"

My sister, Maritza, received a similar note. She had been promoted to Grade 3. No report card, no grades, no indication of how we had done in our courses—just this simple notice. From my perspective, it was a miracle!

## The Garden State

Although Catholic Charities provided us the basics, we still depended on assistance and welfare, and it shamed my father. For months, my parents had watched Maritza and me suffer. My father, a lifelong hard worker, determined to look after his family, decided that we had to move—again.

Our next destination: New Jersey. My uncle had moved from Miami to Union City, New Jersey, and told my father there was work. So, at the end of the school year, "*en cuanto las hojas empezaron a salir*—as soon as the leaves started to appear," my father said, we were to pack our belongings and head to New Jersey, the Garden State.

At first, a former neighbor in Cuba, Tirso Ruano, put us up in his small apartment. When he and his family arrived in the United States, he had stayed with us in Miami. Now he was returning the favor. That's the way it was in the Cuban refugee community in the United States—everyone helped each other. By the time we reached New Jersey, our meager refugee assistance was gone. So, as they had done in Miami, my parents again had to borrow money to rent a new apartment.

In early summer, we settled in West New York, New Jersey, a densely populated industrial town on the banks of the Hudson River, among the New Jersey Palisades. This was not at all like Pittsburgh. It was hot and humid, and people in the streets spoke Spanish! There were Latin shops and movie theaters showing

Spanish-language films. I was so excited to be able to understand what was being said. I could leave the house and not feel like an oddity.

As summer progressed, people began walking around in white athletic undershirts like the ones men wore in Cuba. In the evenings, people sat outdoors on their apartment steps because it was cooler in the street. That reminded me of Cuba. I felt elated. Sure, the landscape was different with its huge buildings and housing blocks, lack of trees, and stifling air, but there was a real sense of community. I hadn't experienced this since prerevolutionary Cuba. At last, it felt like home.

Kids who spoke Spanish congregated in the nearby park, and we talked about our adjustment issues and common problems. And did I talk! For a year or more, I'd lived in virtual silence, except for speaking with my family. I'd felt a bit like a Trappist monk, contemplating life in enforced reticence, speaking only when I was safe and secure inside my own home.

Suddenly, I was part of the group—pick-up basketball, movies, cafés, and more. From the edge of the Hudson River, we could look across at Manhattan. It was thrilling. The number of buildings, the height of the skyscrapers, the hustle and bustle—my life had turned around.

Because of the large influx of Cuban émigrés in the 1960s, our area was known as "Havana on the Hudson" (Bartlett 1977). It was also referred to as the "Embroidery Capital of the World" because of its heavy textile industry, although there were lots of other types of factories and manufacturing plants. With heavy industry came smog. When it rained or snowed, everything turned brown. Even on sunny days you could look across the Hudson River and see a dark cloud hovering over New York City.

At first my mother found work operating heavy machinery in a factory that made leather purses and shoes. Then she switched to a textile factory that was affectionately known as "*La Escuelita*—The Little School." This was the place where practically every Cuban looking for work in the textile industry in West New York cut their teeth. It hired factory workers without experience and taught them how to operate commercial sewing machines, an important skill in the textile industry. Since my mother didn't know how to drive, she took the bus to work, which was difficult for her in the winter. But she eventually found employment in a small, family-run embroidery factory right around the corner from our apartment. She liked it there and told me, "*Los jefes eran unos viejitos muy buenos*—The bosses were very nice old people." They treated her like family and she grew very comfortable there.

By now I was thirteen and starting to discover girls. I enrolled in Public School No. 5, which today is 97 percent Hispanic, and began to make friends. I attended school dances and listened to music by The Platters, The Beach Boys, and Motown artists. I began to be self-conscious. I was terrified that I would be bullied again for being overweight. Charles Atlas came to my rescue. I read his magazines and slimmed down by changing my diet and exercising. I did push-ups between two chairs, and had a metal bar lodged at the top of my bedroom door for pull-ups. My body image improved. I wanted to wear stylish clothes, which made me feel good. I even got a part-time, after-school job in the boiler room of an apartment house. In the summer, I worked with a truck delivery person, taking food and other groceries to New York. I used my earnings to buy clothes, go to the movies, and get other things I needed. My mother and father never asked me to contribute toward the rent.

My new body image, my new clothes, and my growing confidence at school encouraged me when I went to school dances and other social events. It was my coming of age—I was somewhat precocious. But I was more mature than other kids, ready to blossom and become an adult. And I was attractive to girls, some even older than me. My life was really starting to come together, as it was for my family.

My father and Tirso started an auto repair business they named "R&G" (for Ruano and González) and put up a large sign advertising their business: "*Mecánico Cubano*—Cuban Mechanic." Cubans have an international reputation for being great mechanics, enhanced by their ability, since the revolution, to keep the 1950s American cars running in Cuba. R&G was a two-car garage that looked like a small storage warehouse with an aluminum door that lifted up. The tools and smells inside the garage were exactly what I remembered from my father's auto repair shop in Cuba. Metal barrels cut in half were filled with gasoline or other cleaning fluids to soak and degrease auto parts. The heavy fumes mixed with oil and grease created a distinct pungent smell. My father fashioned a fan from a radiator cooling fan, car generator, and tire rim. This helped him keep cool in the summers and pushed out the fumes. Tirso concentrated on body work and helped my father with small engine and brake jobs. My father did the major mechanical work—transmission and major engine repair. It was not a big business, but work was steady and they were making a living. My parents were finally happy. They had found productive work and we were financially secure.

I completed the seventh and eighth grades at Public School No. 5, and for ninth grade moved on to Memorial High School. I was still keeping a low profile and doing only what I had to do to get by. But outside school I had established a social group of Cuban and other Hispanic peers. Among them was Rafael Garcia, a Cuban émigré from Havana. His parents were college-educated and had run a successful pharmacy business in Cuba. We nicknamed Rafael "Batista" after the Cuban dictator because he had an assertive attitude and often wore khaki pants that gave him an authoritarian appearance. Later, Rafael played a pivotal role in my decision to attend college.

Rafael and I were young adolescents struggling to find a sense of identity and adjust to a world that looked and felt very different from what we were used

The R&G auto repair shop in West New York, New Jersey. My father (*right*) stands with his business partner Tirso Ruano after filing ownership papers for their shop.

to. He was dark and handsome with a thick head of brown hair accentuated by a widow's peak. Some facial birthmarks made him self-conscious. He was meticulous about keeping his hair groomed and always carried a small comb. There was a certain sense of competition between us—we tried to outdo each other in hairstyle, clothes, and the girls we were beginning to date. We had different opinions about spirituality and frequently argued about the meaning of life. But we got along well and our friendship deepened. We often spoke about the cars we wanted to drive when we got our licenses, and how we would stand up for each other as high school friends in the face of challenges.

The large influx of Cuban refugees and other Hispanic groups into West New York created ethnic divisions and tensions. The Italians became Wasps and the Hispanics, Spics. If an individual found himself in a confrontation, the group coalesced around him as protection in case of a fight. There were sometimes "rumbles"—a term from *West Side Story*—organized fights between groups. There were gangs of older kids in our neighborhood, with cars, girlfriends, and access to liquor and other drugs. But they couldn't be bothered with the younger kids.

I was getting along well and fitting in with my own group of friends. Then my mother got sick. She had had trouble adjusting to the New Jersey smog and climate and developed severe allergies. After lengthy treatment, the doctors said her getting well required a change of climate. So, three years after we arrived in New Jersey, my parents decided to go back to Miami. My mother was reluctant. Economically we were getting by, she liked her work, and, most important, the difficulties of that first year in Miami were fresh in her mind. But my father insisted that her health was more important.

This decision hit me hard. For the first time in four years, I was part of a community where I belonged. I could walk down the street and not wonder which bully or person intent on ridicule was hiding around a corner. I was on the cusp of becoming a man in a place that accepted me. I knew I could succeed. Now I'd have to uproot and again become a migrant. Each night I went to bed with the words, "Here we go again!"

# 4 Miami Do-Over

My TIME IN New Jersey was a turning point in my development. I felt good about myself for the first time in ages. I'd lost weight; I looked sharp in the clothes I'd purchased with money from my part-time-job; I could speak, understand, and write in English ... and I wasn't afraid of what could happen to me. Perhaps it was this sense of growing confidence that blurred the fact that I was embarking on an identity crisis. On the outside, I was a Cuban American. On the inside, I didn't know whether I was American or Cuban. Regardless, voices in my mind said this was something I could deal with.

Suddenly, it ended. I knew we had to leave New Jersey, and I didn't resent it. I was a child in a loving family and understood why we had to return to Florida. But my foundations were being shaken. Again, I was going back to the state where I'd been bullied, where a harsh, authoritarian vice principal had humiliated me. What would I find in Miami this time? Would I be accepted or again rejected by the Floridian kids, even though I now spoke their language and felt more secure?

In the summer of 1966, right after school ended, we packed our belongings and headed back to Miami. My father had bought a black 1959 Buick Electra 225, which he kept in mint condition. It was a big car and comfortably held the four of us along with everything we owned. It was a long ride and I couldn't keep the memory of being suspended at bay. But as usual, my parents tried to stay positive and reassure Maritza and me that everything would be fine. My father's biggest worry seemed to be getting to "South of the Border," a popular tourist destination along the I-95 corridor, just inside the South Carolina state border. Big signs along the highway proclaimed that "Pedro" was looking forward to welcoming us.

My father kept tabs on how many miles we had to travel before we would get to Pedro's place. He couldn't wait to order the Southern breakfast grits he liked so much. As for me, I just wanted to get my hands on some of the firecrackers Pedro promoted along the highway. I thought it would be great to see all the sparkles and hear a few bangs, just like the old days during the revolution in Cuba!

As planned, we stopped at Pedro's and my father proceeded to indulge his craving with a super-sized serving of grits topped with lots of butter. I spent most of my time in the fireworks aisle engaged in fantasy but had to leave empty-handed as we proceeded on our way to Miami.

With the money they had saved in New Jersey, my parents rented an apartment in a small, two-story building right next to Miami Senior High School.

There aren't that many single-family, two-story homes in Miami—this building was atypical. Built in the 1940s as a single home, it had been converted into a duplex by the owners, who lived on the top level and rented out the lower level. A staircase ran outside the building to the owner's door, providing a private entrance. This white, mildew-stained building across the street from the large, freshly painted Mediterranean-style Miami High stood out like a sore thumb. The practice court for the school's tennis team was right next door to our duplex. Every morning I woke up to the "tac-tac, tac-tac" of tennis balls hitting the court. I could see the players just outside my bedroom window. Going to class was just a matter of walking out the front door and across the street. It was the best place I'd lived in since arriving in the United States.

My father got a job as a mechanic in a service station in Miami proper, and my mother started looking for work in the textile factories in Hialeah, a city just north of Miami. Hialeah had quickly become a manufacturing community, employing and housing vast numbers of Cubans who had settled in the area. The Miami public transportation system was very poor, so there was no way my mother could get from our neighborhood to Hialeah without a car.

She enrolled in an adult education driving school at Miami Senior High School and eventually got her license. But she wasn't comfortable on the road, and recalls being stopped by a policeman who asked whether she thought she was driving "*en el patio de su casa*—in your backyard," because she was going too slowly. He issued a warning and advised her to keep up with the flow of traffic. In time she learned to drive and could get back and forth from Miami to Hialeah to look for work. Because of her experience operating textile machines, she was hired right away. Then she recommended other Cuban friends for employment and offered them transportation to and from work for a share of the commuting expenses.

## Go Stingarees!

Maritza and I were enrolled into our zoned public schools. Maritza started seventh grade at Citrus Grove Middle School, and I started tenth grade at Miami Senior High School. Both schools served the Little Havana area and had large and growing Hispanic populations. Miami High, in particular, was being rapidly transformed, especially by the arrival of new Cuban refugees. Founded in 1903 as a school for whites, it was the first high school in Miami-Dade County. Known as the home of the Miami Stingarees (the school's mascot), Miami High had a rich sports tradition and a history of success. I was headed for a big surprise.

Football was king. Basketball and increasingly baseball were popular sports, but football was the pride and joy of the Stingarees. Football and its traditions were foreign to me. I saw in the main hallway glass cases full of sports trophies commemorating various championships. Pictures of successful student athletes in

The new Miami Senior High School, circa 1930. Photo courtesy W. A. Fishbaugh, used by permission of the State Archives of Florida.

full football gear looked strange to me. Here were these guys with mean-looking scowls and lots of padding, glaring at me in the hallway.

I think the coaches, teachers, families, and even students who were part of the sports culture resented the growing numbers of Cuban students. For years, the school trendsetters had been white Anglo footballers. Suddenly, all these Latin kids appeared, who seemed uninterested in sports, especially football. We must have felt like a plague. Latino newcomers bonded because we felt so alienated. We built our self-esteem by considering ourselves the in-crowd. Those who had lived in Miami for many years were the boring, traditional out-crowd.

School officials tried to make us believe in school traditions. Many Cuban students did take up football and went on to successful careers as student athletes. Trying to fit in, I decided to give it a shot. I made the junior varsity team. I wasn't tall, but I was fast and strong. The coach must have seen potential in me because, from time to time, he let me practice with the varsity team. After practice I limped home in pain from the beatings on the field. Although I worked hard in practice and wanted to perform well on the field, I never fully bought into the mindset that football was the most important thing in the world. That's what the coaches expected.

Outside of football, I was developing a new group of friends with other interests. Among my closest friends were Oscar Tomás Pedraja, a Cuban refugee who had also lived in New Jersey; Arturo Saviñón, a Dominican who had grown up in New York City; Rolando Breto, another Cuban refugee from Miami; and Carlos Rivera, a Puerto Rican living in Miami. Oscar moved down from Elizabeth, New Jersey, the year before I moved back to Miami. He was a good-looking, curly-haired, smooth-talking guy with a flair for embellishing stories. Arturo was tall, tanned, and very skinny. We nicknamed him *"Flaco,"* the Spanish word for "skinny." He lived in Miami with his mother and sister, but had grown up in the rough neighborhoods of New York. He had a quick temper and never shied away from a fight. Rolando, on the other hand, was big and heavy-set, but with a mild personality. I had known Rolando in West New York before our families moved to Miami. Carlos was Arturo's friend before he met the rest of us. He had curly hair and looked like one of the guys in the Sharks, the Puerto Rican gang in *West Side Story.*

The five of us became inseparable. I was the youngest, but the only one with access to a car. As soon as I turned sixteen in September 1966, my father taught me to drive and insisted I get a driver's license. Then he let me drive the 1959 Buick. He never said this, but he probably saw that car as the best defense against inexperienced driving. The Buick was so big and heavy, it was like driving an armored tank with fins. It also had enough room to accommodate all my friends for nights out on the town. On weekends I put on my best clothes and picked up my friends. We were underage, but we usually found a way to get our hands on a few six-packs of beer or sometimes liquor, and did what high schoolers do.

The United States in 1966 was in a period of change. The Vietnam War was escalating and the civil rights movement was intensifying and growing violent. The counterculture movement was underway, the British Invasion was in full swing, marijuana smoking was common, LSD and other psychedelic drugs were spreading, and unconventional hair and clothing styles were catching on. As young Hispanic immigrants, my high school friends and I had to deal with special pressures and questions of identity. On the one hand, we wanted to reject Latino culture and embrace American values. On the other, the United States was not providing clear guidance on just what those values were.

In school, ever mindful of my former suspension, I stayed out of trouble in class, but kept aloof, with little direction for the future. Outside of class, my friends and I adopted American-sounding names: Oscar Tomás became Tommy; Arturo became Art; Rolando became Roland; Carlos became Charlie; and I became Gerry, a name some friends from that era still call me. We let our hair grow and filled our closets with "mod" clothing, including trendy bell-bottom pants and colorful, flowered shirts—styles not tolerated at Miami High, a bastion of tradition and sports prowess. So, by day, we tucked our hair behind our ears, put on our khaki pants and button-down, collared shirts, and went to class. Then, by night, we let our hair down—literally.

That's how I got through my first year at Miami High. When classes resumed in fall 1967, I was promoted to the eleventh grade, but this time placed in a vocational education track. I'm sure that decision was made by well-intentioned teachers who, seeing my lack of motivation and academic interest, didn't think I was college material.

As I had done in all my other classes after the Shenandoah experience, I followed instructions and didn't raise questions. My shop classes, which taught such skills as woodwork and metalwork, were boring, and I had no idea why I was there. But I showed up and went through the motions of learning a trade. I also returned to the football team. This time it was clear I was struggling to meet the coach's expectations and fit in with the team's image. The back of my hair touched the top of my shirt collar, and my sideburns were beyond the acceptable length for a school that frowned upon any break from tradition, especially among athletes.

One day my coach ran into me between classes in the hallway and couldn't resist the opportunity to embarrass me. I had dropped a pass in football practice, and he wasn't happy. So he stopped me in the hall, pinched one of my sideburns between his fingers, and in a heavy Southern accent said, "Shit, boy, you couldn't catch that ball if they put glue on your hands, glue on the ball, and somebody put the ball in your hands. Shiiiit! Get a haircut before you return to practice!"

I realized then and there it would be impossible for me to play sports or fit into the school's traditions. But forces kept me in school; I never considered dropping out. My father's hands and my parents' emphasis on education were vivid reminders of learning as the way to a better life. Even if I didn't understand what getting an education meant, I knew I didn't have many options. Charlie, the oldest in my group, had joined the Air Force after graduation to avoid being drafted into the Army and sent to fight as an infantryman in the Vietnam War. The war weighed heavily on our minds. None of us wanted to go. Except for Charlie, military service didn't interest any of us.

Tommy, to whom I had become very close, had moved out of the Miami Senior High School zone over the summer and was attending Southwest Miami High School. He knew how out-of-place I felt at Miami High and suggested I consider transferring to Southwest Miami, with its more liberal dress code and attitudes. Founded in 1956, Southwest Miami had not yet developed deep-rooted traditions and customs. It seemed like a good fit. For my senior year, I used Tommy's address as my own and started attending Southwest Miami High School.

Located on Eighty-Eighth Avenue and SW Fiftieth Terrace, Southwest Miami was quite a distance from home, but I didn't care. My parents had a new car and had given me the 1959 Buick. It made for early-morning rises, but getting away from what I considered the oppressive traditions at Miami High was worth it.

I saw high school as a necessary evil and just wanted to be done. Southwest Miami offered a co-op program for students who weren't planning to go to college. We could attend classes in the morning and work in the afternoon for the academic credit needed to graduate. Because I had been tracked into vocational education classes at Miami High, it was easy to get into the co-op program. It seemed like a natural placement. Even so, I remained disconnected from the high school experience. I simply wanted to get through the classes I needed to graduate, then get on with my life. I didn't even show up for the yearbook graduation picture.

I got a part-time job at The Rouge in Miami Beach. This small, upscale clothing boutique catered to an affluent, young, professional crowd. Its clothes were among the most stylish and cutting-edge anywhere in South Florida. Customers came all the way from New York and even California. The owner was a young, red-haired, balding Jewish man named Marvin Levine. He was ambitious and very successful. He liked me and offered me a job I could do while enrolled in the school co-op program. I attended classes in the morning, then drove to the boutique to work in the afternoon and early evening. I let my hair grow long and wore avant-garde clothing, including a green velvet-caped suit one of the girls in my fashion merchandising class made for me. This wasn't my first time working in the world of fashion. In Cuba, when I was about nine, I had been asked to model for the store *El Sport Modas Masculinas*—The Sports Men's Fashions—in Placetas for a couple of pesos per session.

I liked working at The Rouge and acquired an appreciation for fine European clothing. I also enjoyed the freedom that comes from earning a few dollars and not being told how to behave. I was a hard worker, and Mr. Levine appreciated my work ethic. He gave me increased responsibility, and I developed a small cadre of customers who sought me out when they came into town to buy clothes. I was turning into a successful retailer; school was the farthest thing from my mind.

Marvin Levine had invested heavily to expand the business and was building a second store, a brand-new two-story building, in an exclusive new area in North Miami. For me, the timing couldn't have been better. The school year was almost over, and we had discussed my becoming a manager or assistant manager in the new store after graduation. Eventually, I would have my own store. My future was all mapped out in my mind. I would become a fashion guru, a salesman of quality clothes to the rich and comfortable. I would dress Miami, then spread my talents by opening my own clothing stores in other parts of Florida and across the United States. My future would be full of fun, fashion, hard work, and enormous rewards—a life of sheer bliss.

But then the economy tanked and the country went into recession. Construction plans were scaled back, worker hours were cut, and I was let go. I was devastated. My dreams, my hopes, and my entire life were suddenly in tatters. Without a business to support me, my vision of a life in retail vanished.

## Batista's Advice

At this time, my friend from New Jersey, Rafael Garcia—Batista—who now attended the University of Puerto Rico, came to visit me in Miami for the summer.

Rafael no longer wore the khaki pants that had earned him the nickname. He was well dressed and had what sounded like clear goals for completing his education and pursuing a career as a pharmacist. He exuded confidence and spoke eloquently about the value of money, the need to manage it well, and his desire to live a comfortable life. In the years since I'd last seen him, Rafael had matured. But I detected a certain emotional emptiness. Did he really believe that achieving all his goals would fulfill him? He clearly wanted to live a life of leisure, but it was also evident that he wasn't thrilled about having to do the hard work needed to achieve it. He wanted to get to his goals as quickly as possible.

But I saw that Rafael valued the education he was getting. He had developed a deeper understanding of human nature than most people I knew. It didn't take him long to realize that I was in despair. Here I was, a new high school graduate, with no job and no idea what I would do with my future. Other than my retail sales experience, I didn't have any marketable job skills. My vocational high school diploma didn't translate into a meaningful trade. Watching my father work so hard all his life, and seeing the long hours my mother was putting in at the factory to make ends meet, I was ashamed at not having a job and a way to independence.

During one of my many deep conversations with Rafael, he said, "Gerardo, why don't you go to college?"

It all sounds so simple to me today. But back then, when my future had suddenly disappeared, it seemed as if God Himself had written the words in the sky: "Why don't you go to college?"

Me? College? I was little more than a high school dropout. I'd been a spectacular underachiever, not motivated to study in any way. I just wanted a certificate so I could leave school and get out into the real world and make something of myself. The idea of continuing my education was so foreign as to be nonsensical. I wanted to put education behind me, not continue it year after year.

But what if Rafael was right? I looked at him in amazement. He was sharp, intelligent, and obviously reveling in the knowledge he was gaining at the University of Puerto Rico. If he could do it, why couldn't I?

He said that he found university to be a stimulating environment, a place of ideas where people from many walks of life came together to learn about themselves as human beings and the world in which they lived. He said some of the students were studying to prepare for careers in pharmacy, teaching, journalism, and the like. Some, he said, were studying humanistic fields such as philosophy, history, and the arts. Yet others were pursuing advanced studies for careers as lawyers, doctors, scientists, and various other professions.

That conversation created a path to my future. Although I didn't fully understand what Rafael was talking about, I was intrigued. Given my options, all of a sudden, college sounded very good.

I knew absolutely nothing about the college application process or what it took to get in. My parents never talked about SATs, GPAs, FAFSA, or any of those other terms associated with going to college. They encouraged me to get an education, but they didn't know how to guide me. When I think of my father's efforts, it's his mechanic's hands I remember. He wanted a better life for me, but he couldn't explain what I needed to do to prepare myself for higher education. And the high school vocational track didn't prepare me, either.

Where would I start? Rafael suggested that I ask about the admission requirements at a local junior college that had recently opened its doors to students who couldn't attend more selective regional and national universities. That summer, after landing on the moon, Neil Armstrong had said going to the moon was "one small step for man ... one giant leap for mankind." I was about to take that leap.

I walked into the admissions office at Miami Dade Junior College and looked around. It wasn't like the moon, alien and strange. I saw colorful posters and brochures and willing people asking how they could help. They explained that junior college was designed to be a transition point between high school and a four-year university program or the world of work. Depending on my goals, and if I completed a two-year course of study, I could earn an associate of arts or associate of science degree. I qualified for admission and applied for the associate of arts program—a path to a four-year degree.

Getting in was the easy part. I had taken the leap. That day changed my life forever.

# 5  I, Too, Am a Passerby

Miami Dade Junior College (later renamed Miami Dade Community College, and now Miami Dade College) had an open-door policy. It began offering classes on what became its North Campus in 1960. From the start, it admitted any student with a high school diploma or a GED. By 1969, when I was admitted, Miami Dade was home to a large and growing number of African American and Cuban exile students who either lacked the grades or the funds to attend other institutions. But even with its low tuition fees, my family and I couldn't afford it on our own. Fortunately, I qualified for federal financial aid under the US Office of Education Loan Program for Cuban Students. This program had been established in 1961 as part of the Cuban Refugee Emergency Center to provide long-term, low-interest loans to Cuban nationals who couldn't receive support from sources within Cuba and who lacked sufficient resources in the United States to pay for higher education (University of Miami, n.d.).

I completed the college placement tests and, unsurprisingly, learned I had some gaps in my education. I knew there would be a lot of ground to make up and obstacles to overcome. But I was motivated and determined. My parents couldn't help me academically, but they taught me the values of hard work and the importance of learning from what life brings. Hard work might sound like a cliché today. But for my family, it was our bedrock. My family history is replete with stories of hard work, resilience, and the desperation of having no opportunity to find meaning in the pride of work.

Though apprehensive, I began my academic coursework willingly and happily. I was especially mindful of my parents' pride. They supported everything I did, even though they didn't understand my choice of courses—mathematics, psychology, philosophy, and other similar subjects. But that didn't matter. What mattered was that their beloved son was working hard and getting an education.

Now that their son was embarking on a college education, they could see that my life was changing. They knew hard work would be my guiding hand. I knew there would be failures, but I would learn from them.

## Family Struggles

My father often told me stories about the challenges his family faced when he was young. Their economic situation was dire. There was no work; there was nothing to do. With tears of shame in his eyes, he told me about a time—he was about six—when his father took him to his cousins' house to see if they could spare an old pair of shoes for my father to wear to school. My grandfather had explained, "*Claro que solo fuimos a pedir, pero no a rogar*—Of course we went to ask, but not to beg." The cousins were three brothers—the youngest, an affluent lawyer. They responded by chasing my grandfather and my father away with a barrage of insults.

One day, my father observed my grandfather cutting a piece of rope "*como el largo de la mesa*—about the length of a table," which he folded and hid in his hands behind his back. My grandfather started to head out of the house, and my father asked, "*¿Adónde vas?*—Where are you going?" My grandfather said he was going to visit some friends. My father insisted on going along. My father knew there was something on my grandfather's mind.

Once they arrived at their destination, the family engaged my father in conversation and distracted him. My grandfather slipped out the back door and across the patio. But my father saw him leave, and a few minutes later, went looking for him. My grandfather had gone into the outhouse that served as a toilet. My father ran to it and flung open the door. He found my grandfather "*amarrado con la soga en el cuello*—with the rope around his neck."

My grandfather was startled. He looked at my father "*y se le salieron las lágrimas*—and the tears ran down his face." With his hands on my father's shoulders, he said, "*Vamos para la casa*—Let's go home." My father said if he had arrived two minutes later, my grandfather would have hung himself. "The situation was so bad," he said. "*Era tan grave. Pero la vida es la vida*—It was a grave situation. But life is life."

After this, my father went wherever my grandfather went, "*como si fuera su sombra*—as if I were his shadow." During one of their outings, they went to the local sugar mill—*El Central Zaza*—to see if they were hiring. Along with El Central Fidencia and El Central San José, it was the main source of employment in Placetas. My grandfather was a *templero*, a skilled worker who specializes in boiling the sugarcane juice to produce raw sugar. As usual, the staff said they were not hiring. Tired from the walk, the two decided to stop and rest. "In a few moments we will continue slowly on our way home," my grandfather told my father. They sat quietly, but my father said, "*Pero yo sí sentía lo que llevaba por dentro*—But I could sense how he was feeling inside." As they continued on, my grandfather suggested that they stop by the Café Rivera, a local coffee shop frequented by many of the town's Spaniards. They sat at "*una mesa cuadradita de bambú*—a small square table made of bamboo." My father said he will never forget it.

One of the Spaniards, whom they called *El Jefe*—The Boss—approached and started a conversation. El Jefe told my grandfather they were having a technical

My grandfather Manolo's work permit photo.

problem at the sugar mill getting the *guarapo*—sugarcane juice—to the right temperature to produce the required quantity of raw sugar. With a pencil, my grandfather drew some diagrams on the bamboo table, showing ways to position the boilers for maximum effect. As my father later explained, "*Oye, eso lo estoy mirando como si fuera hoy. Pintó un tallo, y otro tallo, y otro tallo*—Listen, I can see this as if it were happening today. He drew one detail, and another detail, and another detail." The drawing led to an extended conversation about the solution. Impressed, El Jefe told my grandfather, "You are a great *templero*. Come by El Central Fidencia tomorrow and ask for me."

The next day, with my father in tow, my grandfather asked for El Jefe. After some small talk, El Jefe said, "*Bueno, tú puedes empezar a trabajar ahora mismo—* Well, you can start working right now." My grandfather began to earn a little money and things began to change. "But we went through a big crisis, a very big crisis," my father said. "The problem is that he was the head of a household with a spouse and kids. We needed to eat, we needed to pay rent, and he wanted to send the kids to school."

My grandfather worked at El Central Fidencia until the revolution. Even afterwards, he worked there at night, and by day minded the bodega, a small corner grocery shop he later opened. Eventually, the Castro government nationalized his bodega, but he was still running it and working at El Central Fidencia when we emigrated.

When the sugar mills closed for the off-season, my grandfather did odd jobs to make ends meet. Sometimes he went out into the country for weeks at a time to make charcoal. It's a time-consuming and arduous process that requires constant vigilance. One night everyone in the house woke up to screams outside: "*¡Ayyy! ¡Ayyy! ¡Ayyy! ¡Coño!*" My grandfather stood, rooted to the spot, yards away from the house, screaming in pain. He had walked for miles to save the few cents it would have cost to ride in a taxi. "*Sus pies parecían un par de barriles—*His feet looked like a pair of barrels," my father said. My grandmother, Encarnación, also found seasonal work at a local cigar factory. She was a *plantadora*, a worker who inspects the individual tobacco leaves, sorts them according to quality, and presses them into bundles. Once the bundles are separated, they go to the *engaviador*, the person in charge of starting the process of rolling the leaves into what becomes a cigar. It was tedious work under harsh conditions, but it contributed to the family income during the tobacco harvesting season.

My father's family struggled just to survive. My mother's situation was not as bad. She was part of a large family and lived on a farm. Although there was little money, they grew their own food, and during the sugarcane growing season, made enough money to get by. They endured, doing whatever it took to look out for each other.

From my grandparents' and parents' hardships came a strong work ethic and family values that have persisted through the generations.

## Lessons Learned

In college, it was my time to put those lessons to work. I didn't think of myself as especially intelligent or gifted, but I firmly believed that if I put my mind to it and worked hard at the things I cared about, I could achieve them. Education was changing my mind about myself and my future, and about education itself. Although I still lacked a clear sense of direction, I had become thirsty for knowledge.

I started taking philosophy courses about the great existential doctrines of Søren Kierkegaard, Jean-Paul Sartre, Friedrich Nietzsche, and Albert Camus. I began to read the great books by Miguel de Cervantes and Fyodor Dostoyevsky, debating the meaning of the "I Have a Dream" speech by Dr. Martin Luther King Jr., learning about Albert Einstein's theory of relativity, analyzing the mysteries of Charles Darwin's natural selection, and more. These were difficult subjects and I struggled with some of them. But every failure motivated me to try harder. As I learned more and more, my world view was expanding from the local to the universal. I began to understand where education could take me.

I wasn't alone. Some of my closest friends saw my excitement and realized there could be something in this education thing for them. They, too, enrolled in Miami Dade Junior College. It was as if my life, my circle, and my society were all coming together on an upward path to achievement and success.

## Choosing a Major

While every course looked interesting and challenging, I was undecided about a major. Miami Dade offered a wide array of majors, most of which were unfamiliar. I had heard about the Counseling and Career Services Center that helped students with personal and academic problems. Maybe it could help me sort through my confusion about a major and my future. Walking in, I was apprehensive; I didn't know what to expect. The receptionist directed me to a comfortable waiting room and asked me to fill out a short questionnaire about myself. A counselor greeted me, glanced at my questionnaire, and said, "So you're undecided about majors and not sure where you're headed, right?"

And she was right. Even though I felt the ground growing solid beneath me, quicksand still surrounded me. I was still conflicted about my identity, my status, and my likes and dislikes.

Yes, I explained, I was having difficulty figuring out who I was and what I wanted to do. She listened attentively and suggested a battery of tests could help me with those questions. The tests included a "career interest inventory" that was supposed to reveal how my interests aligned with those of successful people in various occupations.

I had never taken a psychological or career inventory test, so wasn't sure how to answer questions that didn't seem to have a right or wrong answer. The counselor said not to worry about being correct—to simply pick the response closest to how I felt. She also advised that I not spend too much time on any one question.

But the questions were daunting because I was having such a difficult time dealing with my feelings and what I later realized was a deepening identity crisis. Was I really Gerardo or Gerry? How were these two alike and different? What was expected of each? Could I really discard my past identity as a Cuban immigrant in a foreign land that had already taught me some hard lessons? Would I be able to adapt and fit in? I knew I didn't want to be a mechanic. I had watched my father toil so hard for so long. His hands were vivid in my mind's eye. The recession had crushed my plans to become a retail manager. That disappointment was so sudden and unexpected that I rejected the idea of retail as a field of work out of hand. But what would I do?

When I finished the tests, the counselor asked me to schedule another appointment in two weeks to go over the results.

I was excited to learn what the tests had revealed. I thought the counselor would tell me exactly what I was good at and what to major in. But that wasn't the case. Instead, she said my answers indicated that I wanted to help make the world a better place and I enjoyed working with people. Making a lot of money was not a priority.

It came like a bolt out of the blue. But she was right. When Rafael talked about growing wealthy through the family trade as a pharmacist, I knew that was his life, but not mine. Even then, I sensed that I wanted to help people. But until this counselor explained my test results, I'd kept that desire in the back of my mind.

Now it was right smack in front of me. I did want to help people through life's traumas. I was a good listener, and friends often confided in me. I enjoyed listening to them and helping them sort through whatever problems or issues they were dealing with. Money was never an overriding goal. I'd always leaned toward doing things I enjoyed for the intrinsic sense of accomplishment and fulfillment. But except for my conversations with Rafael and the counselor, I had not discussed these feelings with anyone. Still, it was impossible to imagine what would bring me that sense of satisfaction in a course of study.

The counselor showed me a list of occupations that people with similar test scores enjoyed and were good at. Among them was being a clergy member. That didn't resonate. I had been brought up Catholic, but I struggled with questions of spirituality and the meaning of life. Friends and I had often discussed spirituality and pursuing "oneness" with God, but I was more interested in pursuing an inner path to spiritual awakening than devoting my life to helping others achieve it. Besides, I was starting to reject what I understood as the principles of organized religion. So, devoting myself to the priesthood and a life of celibacy didn't fit. I also ruled out other occupations, like firefighter. Then my counselor suggested psychology.

I didn't know much about the field. What did psychologists do? Among my required general education classes was a psychology course on the dynamics of behavior and I was at least familiar with the term. Maybe, if nothing else, a psychology major could help me sort through my emptiness and confusion. The counselor said that to be a practicing psychologist I'd have to attend graduate school. That seemed irrelevant—I was too focused on finding myself and choosing a major to worry about graduate school. My biggest challenge was getting through that first semester and looking ahead to doing something I found rewarding. So, I chose to major in psychology.

## The General Education Curriculum

I was relieved. I enjoyed the material I was learning in my psychology classes and excited to have something concrete to focus on. But why did I have to take all the required courses in the general education curriculum? At the time, that curriculum was designed around the canons of Western civilization, including exposure to the Great Books, as well as contemporary arts, music, drama, and philosophy. It also included natural sciences, social sciences, and English composition. Composition was difficult for me. My spoken English and comprehension had come a long way in the seven years I'd been in the United States. But writing, especially any form of technical writing, required a lot of effort. The words didn't come easily, but I wasn't afraid to write and rewrite a paper, poem, or any assignment until it expressed what I wanted to say.

One memorable writing assignment asked us to find a source of inspiration and write a brief poem following a prescribed format. This was my first attempt at writing poetry. I went to Matheson Hammock Park, a waterfront park just south of Miami, one of my favorite spots to study, and wrote the following:

"My friend the sea, ever changing always constant
The reflection of infinity from its depth came to me
My friend the sea, calm yet mighty to a call of its own
A drop, an ocean
All the same without a friend."

That meant something to me. But my professor didn't see it. He gave me a D. Undeterred, I tried again:

"Onlookers and passersby
Not knowing, not caring but to them what they are
I, too, am a passerby."

My professor thought these words, too, lacked eloquence and poetic prowess. I got a D for the course. No matter—I was learning from my failures.

All my friends at Miami Dade were Hispanic—mostly Cubans. Outside class and at home we spoke Spanish. Mastering English, especially writing the language, was difficult and progress slow. I was doing better in my other classes, especially in humanities and philosophy. I was engaged in reading the Great Books and admiring the arts. Especially inspiring were the words of a popular song: Bob Lind's "Elusive Butterfly." They captured my sense of wonder and search for love.

Where would I find love? Not just the high school kind of puppy love or even carnal love, but transformative love—the kind that gives meaning to life and fills the soul's emptiness. I reflected on the purpose of life, the nature of the universe, and the existence of God.

One of my favorite books was Dostoyevsky's *The Brothers Karamazov*. It resonated with one of my most agonizing struggles: suffering and its role in spiritual awakening. Time and time again I kept coming back to Ivan Karamazov's question in the chapter "Rebellion" about how a just and merciful God could let children, who are without sin and full of innocence, suffer the world's unspeakable agonies. "But then there are the children, and what am I to do about them? That's a question I can't answer," said Ivan (Dostoyevsky 1900, 290). For me, that passage raised deep questions about faith.

My questions were revealing a world of the mind I didn't know existed. I had been comfortable in the beliefs shaped by the world of my childhood. I thought I knew right from wrong. But my studies shook my foundations. The existential philosophies I was studying said finding meaning required action, studying subjects and perspectives that were inconsistent and sometimes incompatible with what I'd been taught.

## The Acculturation Gap

I lived at home with my parents during my first year at Miami Dade. I was becoming even more liberal in my thinking and manner of dress than I had been in high school. I appreciated the fact that no one in college judged my beliefs or cared what I looked like or what I wore. Given my high school experience, that was important. At home, it was a different story. My parents clung to traditional values and traditions rooted in Cuban culture. So, along with the inevitable generation gap, even more striking during the 1960s counterculture revolution, I also experienced an acculturation gap. This is a common phenomenon among immigrant groups when the younger generation acculturates more rapidly than the older one (Birman and Poff 2011).

Nowhere had the gap grown larger than around the topic of religion and spirituality. My parents weren't practicing Catholics or members of organized religion in the traditional sense. But they were devout Christians and deeply spiritual. Because my mother saw motherhood as the central role of women in Cuban society, she was especially devoted to *La Virgen de las Mercedes*—Our Lady of Mercy—whose image is that of the Virgin Mary dressed in white, tenderly holding a child in her arms. I was born on September 24, *El Día de las Mercedes*—the Day of Our Lady of Mercy. That made her even more special in our home.

For Cuban Catholics, every day of the year has a saint, and every saint a Feast Day. It was customary to name children after their Catholic Feast Day saint. Mercedes is a woman's name, so if my parents had named me after her, I would have grown up like the boy in Johnny Cash's popular song, "A Boy Named Sue." Still, my parents would not part with tradition, so they used the shortened version, Merced, as my middle name.

My sister Maritza's Feast Day saint is a male: San Justo, or Saint Just. So, her middle name took the feminine form—Justa.

In Miami, my father had met a practicing member of *Espiritismo*, which is related to the Afro-Cuban underground religion known as *Santería*. Santería originated from the *Yoruba* religion brought to the Americas by African slaves, with some elements of Catholicism imposed by the Spanish masters (Types of Religion, n.d.). When the Yoruba slaves were brought to Cuba, they were forced to convert to Catholicism. Instead of adopting church traditions, they gave African names to Catholic saints and established a unique religion that incorporated deities, known as *orishas*, and rituals from both faiths. For centuries, Santería was practiced in Cuba as an underground religion, originally to avoid sanctions by the Spaniards, and later, due to the general stigma attached to the island's Afro-Cuban culture and traditions. Many Cubans who left the island took their religion with them, and Santería spread to the United States, Canada, Europe, and South America. Today, in Miami and other large Cuban American communities in the United States, many shops, festivals, and rituals are rooted in Santería.

During my return visit to Cuba in 2012, I visited a Santería temple dedicated to *Yemaya*, one of the more popular orishas among Afro-Cubans. A high priest explained his traditions and the history of Santería. I asked how Santería had survived the revolution during the religious repression, when Marxist atheist doctrine was strictly enforced. He explained that Santería had centuries of experience surviving repression by the Spaniards, the Catholic Church, and others in power. In fact, from his perspective, Santería had saved Catholicism in Cuba by keeping alive a form of worship that blended African and European religions. That blend was evident in my home. My childhood home in Miami held certain beliefs and practiced rituals rooted in Catholicism, Espiritismo, and Santería. In our home stood shrines honoring Santa Bárbara, San Lázaro, la Virgen de las Mercedes, and other saints recognized by different orisha names in Santería. My parents made offerings of fresh-cut flowers, clean water, candies, toys, and more. The flowers placed in front of la Virgen de las Mercedes were always white, recognizing her purity. My father was especially devoted to San Lázaro, a popular religious figure in the Cuban culture. In Santería, San Lázaro is called *Babálu Ayé*. He is typically petitioned for relief from poverty, chronic illness, immobilizing pain, and skin diseases.

## A Clash of Cultures

At Miami Dade, I was being influenced by friends and my Eastern philosophy courses. Eastern forms of religion interested me, including the teachings of Meher Baba, the leader of a Hindu form of religion based on the idea that love springs spontaneously from within. Some of my friends had taken part in a drug rehabilitation program based on Baba's teachings. The program taught that drug-induced experiences are as far removed from reality as a mirage is from water. One brochure featured a smiling Meher Baba surrounded by flowery drawings and the phrase "Don't Worry, Be Happy." Under the heading "Meher Baba on Drugs," it proclaimed, "The only real experience is to continuously see God within oneself as the infinite effulgent ocean of truth and then to become one with the infinite ocean and continuously experience infinite knowledge, power, and bliss."

These ideas appealed to me. In my bedroom, I hung posters of the smiling Baba, and I brought home some of his books, along with the beads and ornaments used in the group's religious ceremonies. My parents weren't happy, but they were tolerant.

That changed when my sister started to show an interest in Baba's teachings. In Cuban culture, women are protected and generally stay close to home, under their parents' watchful eye. Fathers are especially protective. Maritza was the apple of my father's eye. Maritza was petite—under five feet tall. The trauma of immigration and her delicate physique made my parents even more protective. As a toddler, Maritza looked like a collector's Dutch Baby Doll with her very light skin, almost snow-white blonde hair, and baby-blue eyes. My parents referred to her as a *papujita*, an endearing Cuban slang term, roughly translated as "a darling little doll."

When my parents saw that my Eastern philosophy ideas were influencing Maritza, they had enough. My father stormed into my room and angrily tore down all my Baba posters and artifacts. He threw them to the floor and cried, *"¡Esto te lo tienes que llevar de aquí!*—You must take this stuff out of here!" No more Meher Baba memorabilia in the house.

It wasn't my intention to influence my sister or go against my parents' wishes, but I was aching to establish my own identity. When my father tore down my Baba posters, I realized it was time to leave home and pursue my own search for spirituality and inner peace, though I didn't know where to find them.

## Falling in Love

I met my future wife, Marjorie Ann Reilly, during my first semester in college. I was dating another girl from Puerto Rico. Between classes, I'd go to the apartment she shared with a roommate. Her apartment complex was close to Trader John's, a local bar popular among college students and other young crowds, including some of my own friends. One afternoon a friend came into my girlfriend's apartment and said with excitement, "Gerry, have you seen the girls that just moved in upstairs? You should check them out!"

I went up to the second floor and knocked on their door. When the door opened, there stood Marjorie, with a bag of potato chips in one hand and a beer in the other. We stood silent, looking at each other, not sure what to say. I broke the silence. "Hi, I'm Gerry."

She said, "I know. I've seen you around campus and showing off outside Trader John's."

I wasn't used to feisty girls like Marjorie. I was used to Latin girls who deferred and spoke meekly to boys. I was in awe that such a different, direct, and beautiful girl had noticed me. Marjorie had deep-red hair, pearl-like skin, and bright-blue eyes. Her shape was lovelier than a model's. There she stood, in front of me, wearing cut-off jean shorts and a tank top. She invited me in and offered me a Pabst Blue Ribbon and some potato chips. We sat on cushions on the living room floor. I didn't care much for Pabst beer or potato chips, but that didn't matter. I stayed as long as I could. Before long, I broke up with my Puerto Rican girlfriend and started dating Marjorie.

Marjorie was born and raised in Philadelphia. Her father's family was Irish, and her mother's, Italian. She had moved to Miami with friends for a summer job before starting college. After our first encounter at her apartment, we were together constantly, although there were occasional periods of separation.

In our second year, we decided to move in together. We rented a small efficiency apartment near Miami's Coconut Grove Peacock Park at the edge of the city's bay. The public park was a popular gathering place for hippies, flower children, anti-Vietnam protesters, and other counterculture groups. The Hare Krishna came every day to chant and distribute free food. This group personified what I was learning in my Eastern philosophy classes and my readings. And I was trying to make ends meet. So, the gatherings and free food met two needs. I joined the sect.

Marjorie didn't take kindly to this. I explained I wanted only to be what the anthropologist Margaret Mead called a "participant observer." Still, she wouldn't have it. At night, after the Krishna group finished chanting and distributing food, Marjorie came to the Krishna house—the Krishna Temple, as we called it—and camped out on the front lawn. The group wouldn't let her in, but they couldn't get rid of her.

At the temple, the Krishna leader explained that reaching Nirvana was like carrying a load of rocks and getting rid of them, one by one. He claimed Marjorie was one of the biggest rocks I had to drop. That never happened. I left the temple and carried on with my studies and my girlfriend.

Getting so deeply into Eastern religions and philosophy and my short time with the Hare Krishna were significant experiences. As a participant-observer, I saw firsthand how people can perform unfamiliar rituals and follow dogma, simply in hopes of fulfilling an inner emptiness. I learned there are multiple ways of looking at the world and finding meaning. I began to understand how others could be deeply attached to beliefs so different from mine. It taught me to respect differences.

Marjorie and I having fun in Miami, circa 1972.

## Staying in Touch with a Friend

My friend Rafael stayed in touch when he returned to Puerto Rico to continue his studies. During holiday breaks and during the summer, he visited me in Miami. As we had done in New Jersey, we engaged in long philosophical debates about our different world views, faith, and the meaning of life. We disagreed on life's higher purpose, but our arguments were always based on well-reasoned beliefs that were worth contemplating.

With his professional, upper-middle-class background in Cuba, Rafael was much more attuned than I to the role of money in achieving goals. His highest priority in getting an education was landing a good job and accumulating wealth. His goal of being a pharmacist was largely driven by the salary expectation he had for that profession. His studies focused on the sciences, with few opportunities for liberal arts and exploratory courses. But he, too, struggled with questions of identity. Between visits, Rafael stayed in touch through letters.

In a letter dated Sunday, September 19, 1971, five days before my birthday, Rafael expressed angst about his future. His letter was written inside a birthday card that featured a well-known quote from Henry David Thoreau:

> "If a man does not keep pace with his
> companions, perhaps it is because he hears
> a different drummer. Let him step to the music
> he hears, however measured or far away."

Rafael told me many things. He was winding up his pharmacy studies and would soon embark on his profession. He was taking three credits of psychology and with an extra semester could receive an additional bachelor's degree in psychology. Maybe that could serve as a foundation for studying law, which could be useful in serving the Latin community in the United States. Where was I going to continue my studies? He reminded me it was important to prepare for a high-income field. He was growing distant from his father for no other reason than destiny, and hoped I still felt warm toward my family. At university, he had met and fallen in love with Isabel, a Mexican girl.

Then he wished me a happy birthday and said, "*En mi existe una parte de ti—* In me there's a part of you." He went on, "I have learned much with you." He tried to learn something from every person he met, and of me, he said, "*Tú has sido una influencia positiva—*You have been a positive influence." He continued, "*Te recordaré en tiempos remotos, pues lo que se ama no se olvida—*I will remember you in the distant future, because you can't forget what you love."

Rafael had also been a positive influence on me. He had shown me the way to college and encouraged me to continue my studies. He had been my best friend in the United States and shown me a different perspective on what is important in life. Our discussions on material wealth versus spiritual wellbeing were deep and always enlightening. He saw education as the path to material gain and the good life. I saw it as a way to know myself, and find a way to fill my unexplained emptiness. It brought immediate rewards—a deeper understanding of human nature and of myself.

Marjorie and I also discussed what we wanted in life and for our future. She was concerned, but not obsessed, with financial security. We had fun. On one memorable occasion, a friend of mine designer of flower arrangements invited her to model for a national competition at the famed Doral Beach Hotel in Miami

Beach. Designers from around the country were exhibiting elaborate flower arrangements. My friend dressed Marjorie as Marie Antoinette. On her head she wore his magnificent arrangement of orchids and other exotic flowers. He won first place. I don't know how much money he received for the prize, but Marjorie didn't get a penny. We didn't care; Marjorie and I celebrated and laughed all the way home. We didn't have any money, but we didn't have a care in the world. We were in love.

## A Question of Priorities

Whenever our conversations turned to money and what we'd need to live comfortably and securely, I told Marjorie the story of a place in my Cuban hometown of Placetas. The central Cuban highway—*La Carretera Central*—went through town, over some dirt roads and unkempt fields. Under that overpass, homeless, destitute people lived in shacks. The place was known as *"El Elevado."* Entire families lived in makeshift houses pieced together with scrap wood, cardboard, and dirt. I told Marjorie that if nothing else panned out, we could always live under El Elevado. She never forgot that story. During one of our separations, she sent a newspaper photo of a similar shanty town set up by Haitian immigrants under the Miami I-95 bypass. She wrote, "I wonder what life under the bridge would be like. I love you always—miss you."

Discussions with my friends and future wife were key to my development. With my school books and lectures, they were fundamental in shaping my thinking and ways of looking at the world. I could not have engaged in such existential questions without my liberal arts education. I didn't know it then, but in the United States, the purpose of a liberal arts education was an old debate. Did it prepare one for a job, or for life? Thomas Jefferson and Benjamin Franklin took opposite sides. Jefferson saw the liberal arts as essential for lifelong learning and democracy. Franklin criticized them as impractical and elitist (Roth 2014).

This debate was fundamental to Western civilization itself. Socrates's dictum that a life unexamined is not worth living was the premise behind a liberal arts education. That education was my springboard to examining my own life and becoming a lifelong learner.

As I wound up my studies at Miami Dade, I wrote a letter to my grandfather in Cuba. I knew he would be proud to know I was soon to get an associate of arts degree, the first college degree in our family. He replied, saying he prayed to God *"que te veas premiado en tus estudios con un título tan grande como ese—*that you'd be gifted in your studies with a title so grand as you're about to receive." He continued, *"Necesario para hacer tu felicidad futura—*Necessary to build your future happiness." He concluded, *"Quiera Dios tengas en el futuro el fundamento necesario, orgullo de tus padres y de tus abuelitos Yeya y Papo, como nos decías—*I hope to God that in the future you have the necessary discipline, and pride in your parents and your grandparents Yeya and Papo, as you used to call us."

I had never been more proud of my parents and grandparents. College had opened my eyes to the big questions. My family's sacrifices had made it all possible. Yes, there were challenges ahead, but I had reached the first milestone.

For the first time in my life, I could see a way forward. In two miraculous years I had learned that for me education was its own reward ... not wealth, or status, or advancement.

There was no way—no way in the world—I was going to stop now!

# 6  Home of the Gators

When I finished Miami Dade College in the summer 1971, I knew I wanted to continue my studies in psychology, but I still didn't have a clear idea about a career I could pursue with that major. I was also uncertain about where I would go for the next phase of my education. Going out of state was out of the question. In Florida, students with a junior college degree were eligible for admission as transfer students to any campus of the State University System. At first, I thought I wanted to stay in South Florida, close to my family and friends and the Latin community. I considered attending Florida Atlantic University, a new state university in Boca Raton, just a few miles north of Miami. But I decided to transfer to the state's flagship university in Gainesville, the University of Florida (UF). Marjorie stayed in Miami to work.

In January 1972, I moved to Gainesville for the winter term. This was "home of the Gators"—the university's alligator mascot. This was also "cracker country," a term especially applied to rural white Southerners. Gainesville was a small agricultural community more like parts of Georgia and other places in the Deep South than the Florida I knew in urban Miami. It might as well have been a foreign country. I saw people in pick-up trucks with shotguns displayed in the back windows, something I'd never seen before. I learned that the locals were called "rednecks." Working in the fields in T-shirts exposed the back of the neck to the hot Florida sun. The Southern drawl I heard everywhere reminded me of the football coach who'd pulled my sideburn at Miami High. It was hard to understand.

The semester before starting at UF, I'd taken a battery of upper-division course-placement tests. I scored below average in verbal ability, in the lower 25 percent of college-goers. I scored in the lower 10 percent for reading ability, but I was in the average range in reading comprehension and speed. I don't know how those scores compared to other non-native speakers of English, but reading and writing were still a struggle. I was much better in quantitative ability, scoring in the upper 75 percent. My overall score was in the average range, just below 50 percent.

My junior college grades were good enough, and I was sure I could succeed at a major four-year institution. But I wasn't ready for the culture shock.

At Miami Dade, all my friends were Latinos. The culture outside class and in the community was decidedly Latin. At the University of Florida, it was very different. I was assigned to live in the dorms with an American roommate from rural northern Florida. Pets weren't allowed, but he snuck in a boa constrictor that roamed the room. He fed it live mice. I wasn't used to seeing that. The toughest thing, however, was not hearing Spanish or seeing other Hispanic students. I felt disconnected.

During orientation and class registration, students stood in long lines, holding their hole-punched computer cards. As I waited in line for registration, I heard a couple of students ahead of me speaking Spanish—the first time I'd heard Spanish on campus. I couldn't pass up the chance to reach out and introduce myself. They welcomed me into the conversation and we had a nice chat in Spanish. We exchanged contact information. That evening I received a call from Juan, one of the Spanish-speakers, who, like me, had transferred from Miami Dade.

Juan and his family were from Havana. He was shy and, unlike most UF students and Gainesville locals, wore bell-bottoms and other clothes popular in the more urban environment of South Florida. He was dark and had long, curly black hair. Juan and I became inseparable. We ate lunch together at the cafeteria, hung out between classes, went out on weekends, and often rode down to Miami to see friends and family. In fact, we went to Miami as often as we could. We missed its Latin culture. We joked that during the UF Homecoming Weekend—a major production in Gainesville—we just went home.

Gainesville was not a diverse community and the UF campus was decidedly white. We had a hard time fitting in. Like many other Southern institutions, UF was under a federal desegregation order that required increasing the number of African Americans and documenting their academic progress. But the desegregation order didn't extend to Hispanics. We were a small group—mostly Cubans—and not officially recognized as a minority group. So, there were no special services to recruit or help Hispanic students adjust to campus. We were back in the "sink-or-swim" mode some of us had experienced in Miami schools when we arrived as Cuban refugees.

Juan and I pretty much kept to ourselves. In Miami, many other Cubans had extended helping hands to their fellow refugees. In Gainesville, we had to find our own way. Juan didn't make it. After the first semester, he decided not to come back.

## A Caring Mentor

Difficult as it was, especially without Juan to commiserate with, I wanted to stay. I wasn't receiving financial aid or special services from the university, but I continued to benefit from the Cuban Refugee Student Loan Program. I also qualified for the Federal Work-Study Program, which offered me a part-time student assistant position in the psychology department. The department was large and had its own building—one of the newest on campus. It was far from the library and main classroom buildings and sat atop a hill, overlooking the immense teaching hospital and medical complex that dominated the southern border of the campus. The university's Institute of Food and Agricultural Sciences used the fields across the street for plant research. In the summer, large tracts of land full of bright-yellow sunflowers adorned the landscape.

My job in the psychology department was to provide clerical assistance to the office staff who supported faculty. I spent a lot of time duplicating and organizing copies of class materials and helping faculty with research-related clerical work. Even in my marginal role, I was working in my major area, learning from leaders in the field about various branches of psychology. If I went back to another college in Miami, I knew I wouldn't have the same opportunities.

My first two psychology courses were taught by Dr. Carol Van Hartesveldt, a young assistant professor who'd been hired to develop a physiological psychology program, which was new to the department. She was tall and thin, with shoulder-length, curly reddish hair. She was not quick to laugh and generally interacted with students and colleagues in a serious, businesslike manner. She wasn't easy to approach, but she had a reputation as a very good teacher and researcher. Students tended to avoid her courses because they were rigorous, but I was interested in learning about the effects of drugs on behavior. So, in my first semester, I signed up for her classes PSY 532—Drug Use and Abuse and PSY 530—Molecular Basis of Behavior.

These were advanced courses. But I was motivated, partly because I had seen so many friends in Miami destroy their lives with illicit drugs. I wanted to know what I could do about it. Why hadn't I gotten involved or addicted, when so many of my friends with similar backgrounds and characteristics had? This question perplexed me, and I wanted to learn as much as I could about the factors that influence addiction to alcohol and drugs.

Dr. Van Hartesveldt knew I was hardworking and motivated but could tell I was struggling with language issues and having difficulty adjusting socially. Dr. Richard Swanson, a social psychologist and attorney, was also new. He was from Colorado, with a Western flair. Like Dr. Van Hartesveldt, he was tall, with reddish hair. He wore a thick red mustache and rimmed glasses, which accentuated his youthful appearance. He was a jovial fellow, with a ready smile. The two were social friends. Dr. Hartesveldt knew Dr. Swanson enjoyed the Latin culture, was fluent in Spanish, and missed speaking the language. She introduced us.

Dr. Swanson and I hit it off. We spent hours talking about the intricacies of Latin culture, and whenever we could, chatted in Spanish. As part of my work-study assignment, I sometimes helped him organize and format his research data on the corrections system and the communities that inmates form. I wanted to combine my interest in drug abuse with his research on corrections. He liked my idea of studying the differences in prison communities formed by those with drug-related offenses and by those charged with more traditional crimes. He agreed to supervise me for an independent study course on the subject.

I was thrilled. I was working with him on meaningful research. And he was interested in me as a person.

On a personal level, this was an especially difficult time. I was lonely. I missed Marjorie, and it was my first time living away from my family in another town. Miami was 300 miles away. But I was under the wings of Dr. Van Hartesveldt and Dr. Swanson. They encouraged me, academically and personally. We grew closer. He was now Dick, and she was Carol. At his invitation, I often joined Dick and Carol for dinner at his house. Our conversations were fun and interesting.

Academically, Dick saw that I struggled with writing and understood why. He was patient and helped me get through multiple assignments that required written and oral skills. I remember fondly, and with some embarrassment, a meeting where I reported on my drug-abuse findings. A term for trying to kick an addiction without medication is to go "cold turkey." I was trying to make the point that in prison many addicts have to withdraw this way; I said they went "cold duck." The group looked at me strangely; some smirked. Dick stayed serious and said, "You mean cold turkey, don't you?"

Indeed, that's what I meant!

Dick was a caring mentor and friend. My relationship with a faculty member who took a personal interest in me and spoke my native tongue was a stroke of luck. Juan and other Latino friends were not so lucky. They didn't or couldn't form such relationships and ended up dropping out. My relationships with Carol and especially Dick allowed me to persevere in college and changed my life.

## Tough Times

Getting by financially was a struggle, too. The Cuban refugee student loan and work-study assistance were barely adequate. After my first semester at UF, Marjorie moved to Gainesville, and we rented a small, inexpensive one-bedroom, one-bathroom house near campus. It was white with black trim, sat on cinder blocks, and had a tin roof. Its kitchen was tiny and the living room could barely accommodate a small sofa and a chair. In the bathroom stood a large antique iron bathtub, but no shower. Next to the house was a large kerosene tank that fueled our home's single heating unit. A small window air conditioner cooled it in summer, but we saved money by sitting under a tree on a wooden bench just outside the front door. Yes, our house was small, but it was cozy.

Ours was a rural neighborhood—a neighbor raised quail for a living. One day a couple of pick-up trucks pulled up to his property and started loading his quail cages. I asked what was happening, and he replied that the city had gotten too big for him and things were getting much too expensive.

Although from my Miami perspective Gainesville didn't seem big, the cost of living was going up. Small and inexpensive as our house was, the rent was higher than I was paying in the dorm. I considered getting rid of my car, but

Our first house as a couple in Gainesville.

I couldn't stand the idea of not being able to jump in the car and head for Miami when I felt the urge to visit family and immerse myself in the Latin culture. Also, Marjorie was waiting tables part-time in a new restaurant on the south side of town and needed transportation.

We couldn't afford movies, restaurants, or other forms of entertainment. Each night, we counted Marjorie's tips and saved them in a jar. Her tips helped a lot, but we still couldn't meet all our expenses.

My parents had visited us a couple of times in Gainesville and were proud of us and encouraging. We were making it on our own, and I was continuing my studies. But they knew we were struggling. They liked Marjorie very much and felt sorry about her long hours at work.

Then my father had an idea. He bought old broken-down cars and worked on them in his yard at night and on weekends. He looked for cars he knew would appeal to a young college population. He fixed everything the car needed—the engine, transmission, electrical system, upholstery, and whatever else—to look and run as if it had just come from the showroom. Then he'd give me the car to sell. When a car was ready, I took the train to Miami on a Friday, my sister or a friend met me at the station, and I spent the weekend at home. Then I drove back on Sunday and, back in Gainesville, put a "For Sale" sign on the car. The cars were in such great shape they usually sold to the first person who looked. I remember a little red Fiat my father bought for under fifty dollars. He restored every single gadget to its original condition. The car looked brand new. I sold it in two days for 700 dollars.

When I sold a car, I sent my father what he paid, plus the cost of parts, and kept the rest. I don't know how Marjorie and I could have gotten by without my father's help. That extra income made it possible to stay in college.

Still, it was tough. Jobs were scarce in Gainesville and Marjorie couldn't find full-time work. Meanwhile, Disney World had opened in Orlando and the city was growing rapidly. So, Marjorie and I decided she'd find work in Orlando while I finished school. I moved in with some roommates, which helped with housing costs. From then on, when I went to Miami to pick up a car, I stopped in Orlando.

## Graduation Day

Finally, the big day arrived. At the end of the spring term in 1973, I received my last grade report with the notation: "Received the degree Bachelor of Arts June 9, 1973." I also received a certificate signed by the university's then president Stephen C. O'Connell. I earned a four-point grade-point average for the quarter and made the President's Honor Roll.

Commencement. June 9, 1973. Under the watchful eyes of my parents, my sister, and Marjorie, I walked across the stage to receive my bachelor's degree and shook hands with President O'Connell. All day long, I thought about the people, places, and events that had made possible my college education.

First of all, I thought about the sacrifices of my parents and grandparents. They were my motivation and my support. They made it clear that for poor families, refugees, and immigrants like us, education paved the way to a better future.

Maritza, or Mari, as our family called her, had started at Miami High and, like me, was struggling with her own identity issues. She and I had been through a lot of school issues together. She had a close-knit group of Latin friends and was doing well in school. She had always looked up to me, and on graduation day, I was acutely aware of her gaze. I felt her pride in seeing me graduate.

I also thought about Rafael and how his visit in the summer of 1969 had set me on a path I didn't know existed. I knew I was fortunate at such a time of

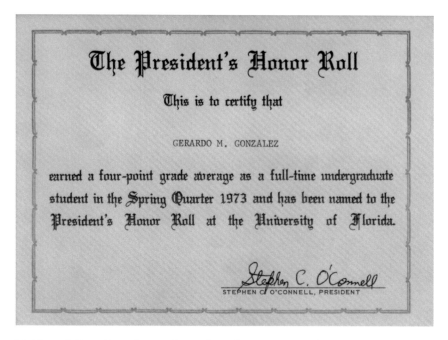

My Honor Roll certificate from my last undergraduate semester at the University of Florida.

transition and even despair to have a friend who reached out with guidance. If it hadn't been for Rafael, I might never have considered college.

I was grateful for Miami Dade Junior College. The low-cost, open-door community college that served minority students, particularly Hispanics and African Americans, had been indispensable. I wasn't prepared for college, and without the start Miami Dade gave me, I couldn't have gone on to a selective institution of higher learning. In college at Miami Dade, I learned about college.

The need-based federal financial aid I received through the loan program for Cuban students had been critical. Without it, even a low-cost institution like Miami Dade would have been out of reach. As for repaying the debt, I thought: I'll figure it out. The important thing was that no one—not Fidel, not the US government, not the banks, not politicians—could ever take away my education. Somehow, I'd make good on my promise to repay the loans.

What made me so sure that if I worked hard, I'd succeed? The image of my father's hands, soaked in grease and marked by a lifetime of toil. His can-do attitude and unorthodox form of encouragement helped me persevere. I didn't see myself as especially intelligent, but a liberal arts education awoke in me a thirst for knowledge and lifelong learning. When I failed, I tried to learn from my mistakes. With each new insight, each new understanding, I grew more motivated.

Standing in my graduation robe before the University of Florida Spring Commencement Ceremonies, 1973.

I thought about Professor Dick Swanson and the many hours we'd spent together at the University of Florida and in Gainesville on academics or socializing and chatting in Spanish. He supported me as a student and as a person. He introduced me to his research in my academic area. Without him, I'd have followed the path of so many Hispanic students like Juan and dropped out.

Then there was Marjorie. Even when we were physically apart, she was there for me, offering love, encouragement, and support. Despite all the fun and excitement of living on a large residential campus, college can be a lonely experience. I had someone who cared. We weren't married, but she was part of the family. I thought: tonight we will celebrate together, and who knows, we may not have to live under El Elevado after all.

On graduation day, I wasn't thinking beyond the bachelor's degree. But I knew that somehow I'd continue to learn and build on this foundation of knowledge. Commencement truly was a beginning, not an end.

# 7  Life After College

My first job after college was assistant director of an experimental group home that served the needs of eight to ten adolescent and pre-adolescent male foster children. For one reason or another, the boys couldn't live with their parents and couldn't be placed in regular foster homes because of a range of emotional and behavioral problems. Some had committed petty crimes, but none serious enough to warrant judgment as a juvenile delinquent. I learned a lot from those boys.

Established by the Florida Department of Health and Rehabilitative Services Division of Family Services, the home was in an old remodeled Victorian house on the east side of Gainesville, a few miles from the University of Florida campus. The director and her husband were live-in residents in the main part of the house. I lived in separate lodgings behind the main structure. When the director or I had time off—not often—the other had to remain on the premises.

A social worker, licensed mental health counselors, and family therapists worked with the boys individually and with their families. I counseled and provided guidance to the boys, but mostly I was expected to be a "big brother" and friend they could confide in. I was supposed to remain impartial and avoid emotional attachment, but I grew very fond of them, especially Cody, Jamie, and Bobby (pseudonyms). I remember them well. Cody was an athletic, articulate, and very smart African American adolescent. In school, he had been academically successful and well-liked. After a fairly normal childhood, he accidently found out that he had been adopted. He rebelled and grew angry; his adoptive parents lost control. He wouldn't accept other foster parents. All he wanted to do was reach legal age so he could be on his own.

Jamie was a big, burly country boy with a heart of gold. When he could no longer live with his natural parents, attempts were made to place him in foster homes, but they failed. If Jamie didn't like something, he came at it with force. Given his size and strength, he could be intimidating. I remember playing tackle football with the boys on the front lawn. Jamie knew he could easily run over me if he came straight ahead with the ball under his arm and pushed his body into mine. He didn't know that in football, a defender could bring down such a runner by lowering his shoulder to the runner's knee level. As he ran toward me at full speed, I looked into Jamie's eyes and saw his determination. Waiting for him to get close, at just the right moment, I lowered my shoulder. Jamie hit the ground hard. He got up, threw the ball as far as he could, and came at me, throwing punches. I had to use all my skills to calm him down. No foster parent could possibly have put up with such behavior.

Bobby was short and overweight, and for most of his life, had been abused and bullied. To cope, he became passive-aggressive. He tattled on the other boys and constantly sought the director's approval. She'd become a sort of surrogate mother to him. When Cody and the others got frustrated by his antics, they ripped into him. That made Bobby even more aggressive. He'd fire off a cycle of whining and complaining, which then led to more verbal and sometimes physical abuse by the other boys. This pattern of behavior would have occurred in Bobby's foster homes, especially if siblings were involved.

I empathized with Bobby. As a child in Cuba, I was overweight and regularly suffered verbal and sometimes physical abuse. The bullying got worse after the revolution, when families unsympathetic to the new government were targeted for all kinds of harassment. I remember being afraid and at least once being punched in the face by older neighborhood kids. The thought of escaping that abuse made me less apprehensive about emigration. I didn't realize my parents knew about the bullying and were concerned about my weight. In my home, eating a lot and being overweight were signs of "*buena salud*—good health." Years later my father pulled medical records from an old file showing that after I turned eleven, he and my mother took me to the doctor in Santa Clara to check on my weight problem. I was shocked.

At that time I weighed 104 pounds and was fifty-five inches tall (four feet, six inches). The average weight for kids my age was seventy-three pounds; the average height, fifty-three inches (four feet, four inches). The normal weight for a child my size was eighty-five pounds. The doctor prescribed a diet. For breakfast at 7 a.m. I had "*un vasito de leche con café*—a small glass of milk with coffee," a small glass of fruit juice, and a poached egg. At 10 a.m. I could have a piece of fruit without sugar. At noon I could have lunch, but no "*arroz, harina, frijoles, salsa, carne de cerdo, dulces, o pasta de sopas*—rice, flour, beans, salsa, pork meat, dessert, or pasta." A snack at 4 p.m. consisted of fruit or a glass of milk. At dinner at 7 p.m. I had salad, soup, beef, and a small dessert. I wasn't supposed to drink water with meals or before I went to bed.

With a diet like that, it's hard to imagine how much I had been eating before. Maybe the stress of bullying made me overeat. Bobby certainly ate to deal with stress.

Seeing Bobby struggle revived my own painful childhood memories. I felt bad for all the kids. They were good kids who'd been dealt a bad hand. Ivan's question about the children in *The Brothers Karamazov* resonated in my mind: "But then there are the children, and what am I to do about them?"

All I could do was treat them with dignity and respect. Family disruption and anger—lots of anger—were common in these young lives. I assumed it sprang from the neglect and abandonment kids experience when there's no family security or love. Pre- and early adolescence had been especially hard for me, but my family's focus on staying together had helped me get through the hardships. Why did these kids have such a different experience? It wasn't their fault they'd grown up without parents and under such difficult circumstances. It was gut-wrenching to try to help these kids manage their anger. And it was almost impossible to emotionally detach.

## Doing What You Love

I wanted to do more for these kids. Maybe with proper training I could do a better job helping them cope. What about graduate school? If I knew more about counseling and how to reach the boys, maybe I could be more helpful. After four months at the group home, I prepared my application materials for graduate school. In my application I wrote, "I am interested in working with people, particularly pre-adolescent and adolescent children who are in need of counseling and guidance in their personal and social development.... [N]ow more than ever I realize the need to complement my work with graduate training."

Finding something I loved was key to doing it successfully. I recalled many conversations with my father about how he found his passion for being an expert mechanic. He'd explained his career trajectory in detail. Circumstances made him entrepreneurial at an early age. At the age of seven or eight, he asked the town milkman if he needed help delivering milk. He was hired. Every day at the crack of dawn, before school, my father waited for the milkman at the edge of town to collect containers of milk to deliver. He also convinced several of his milk delivery customers to let him fill their water tanks for a few extra pennies. Many homes in Cuba depended on water pumped into tanks that sat on roofs. My father got 30 cents for each tank he filled. But he was especially proud of a job he created cleaning shoes. He perfected a technique for making white shoes— in vogue among the town's prostitutes and playboys—shine to perfection. He recalled, "*Y me hice de clientes todas las putas y chulos que vivían allí*—And I had as clients all the prostitutes and playboys who lived there."

In adolescence my father decided it was time to learn a more honorable trade. He seemed to have an affinity for shoes, so my grandfather, Manolo, took him to his shoemaker friend, Alberto, and asked him to teach my father the trade.

"In those days entrusting a son to a tradesman to learn his trade was like a sacred pact," my father said. To Alberto, my grandfather said, "*Oye, aquí lo tienes y él es tuyo*—Listen, here he is and he is yours." Every day after school, my father went to Alberto's shop to learn the arduous process of putting 200 to 300 small nails in the soles of the shoes. Alberto showed my father how to put the nails in his mouth, place the shoe on his knee with the sole facing up, and hammer away. Every day he came home with a huge black-and-blue mark on his leg in the shape

My father doing the work he loved best—repairing a car engine.

of a shoe. He said, "*Posiblemente los problemas que hoy tengo en la pierna sean de eso*—It is possible that the problems I have with my legs today came from that."

My father wasn't meant to be a shoemaker. So he asked Manolo's permission to try something else. Manolo asked Castel, a local carpenter who made furniture, to teach my father his trade. Castel replied, "*Bueno que venga para acá; lo voy hacer carpintero*—Well bring him over; I'll make a carpenter out of him." But my father couldn't handle the dust. Every day he left the shop covered from head to toe with dust: "*Así blanco de polvo*—Completely white from the dust," he recalled. "*Esto tampoco es para mí*—This is not for me either."

On his own, my father decided to be a mechanic. He remembered an old man in town who had a small auto repair and welding shop: "*Un mecánico viejo del pueblo con mucho conocimiento de los carros de aquel tiempo*—An old mechanic in town who had a lot of knowledge about cars from that era," he recalled. The old man let my father come by every day after school and observe. He wasn't allowed to work on the cars, but he could watch and ask questions. "*Miraba cómo hacía eso y esto. Todos los dias iba por allí*—I would go and watch how he did this and that. Every day I would go there." When he felt he knew enough, my father started welding and fixing cars. He explains, "*La herramienta que no tenía la hice*—The tools I didn't have I made." So, "*Me hice mecánico*—I became a mechanic."

After secondary school—equivalent to having an eighth-grade education—he opened his own auto repair and welding shop. "*Así empecé*—That's how I started," he recalled. "*Nunca se me olvida lo que aprendí alli*—I'll never forget what I learned there."

Graduate training would require a big commitment on my part. I wanted to pursue it with the same passion and dedication my father had pursued becoming a mechanic.

## Admission to Graduate School

In October 1973, I applied for admission to the University of Florida Graduate School in the field of counselor education. My Graduate Record Examination scores were not stellar: 390 in the verbal section and 540 in the quantitative section. But my reference letters were good, and my undergraduate grades progressively strong. That convinced the admissions committee. On December 20, 1973, I received a letter from the assistant dean of the College of Education saying that I'd been admitted to the graduate school for the winter semester of 1974. In January, I began my studies toward the master's and education specialist degrees in counselor education. I attended part-time while continuing to work in the group home. I wanted to use with the boys everything I was learning about active listening, unconditional positive regard, empathy, and other counseling skills. But working full-time in that intense emotional environment while pursuing a course of graduate studies was too much. At the end of the summer of 1974, I resigned from the group home to dedicate myself full-time to graduate school.

There were also personal reasons for resigning. Being a live-in assistant director wasn't easy. When Marjorie came to visit in Gainesville, she had to sneak into my living quarters so no one would get upset. I wasn't allowed to have visitors, especially a girlfriend, and we couldn't afford to rent a place for the weekends. Marjorie and I had started to think about marriage. The group home arrangement made it difficult to plan our future life.

## The Graduate Assistantship

In the fall of 1974, I was offered a graduate assistantship in the University of Florida's Office for Student Services. I became an administrative assistant to the dean of students, Dr. Thomas Goodale. At first, I handled general administrative duties like short-term advising and student withdrawal counseling, preparing feasibility studies, coordinating research efforts in the office, and generally helping with student affairs programs. I enjoyed working with college students and was learning a great deal from Dean Goodale's supervision and mentoring. It was a wonderful introduction to the field of college student personnel services and a great opportunity to combine my counseling interests with administrative skills.

In November 1975, Dean Goodale was invited to a meeting at Notre Dame to review the contents of the *Whole College Catalog About Drinking*. This publication grew from an initiative sponsored by the National Institute for Alcohol Abuse and Alcoholism to gather and disseminate information about alcohol use and abuse among college students. Its goal was to bring these issues to the attention of universities and stimulate education and communication to prevent alcohol-related problems (Hewitt 1977).

Dean Goodale was on the catalog's editorial board. As dean of students, he was all too familiar with the devastation alcohol abuse wreaks on college campuses. He'd grown up with an alcoholic brother, so he had both a professional and a personal interest in the topic. He was also aware of my interest in the subject of alcohol and drug abuse. When he returned to Florida, he asked me to take the lead in developing an alcohol education program at the University of Florida.

This was an exciting challenge. Many of my friends in Miami and some at the University of Florida were seriously involved with alcohol and other drugs. Some had ended up in jail, and others fared even worse. The question "Why not me?" was still on my mind. Working on the problem was a chance to explore the issue in a new way.

My first task was to dig into the research on campus alcohol abuse and learn as much as I could. I was surprised that, despite the widespread use of alcohol and its serious effect on college students, research was scarce. Most of the literature focused on the disease of alcoholism and on Alcoholics Anonymous. Nevitt Sanford's 1967 classic volume, *Where Colleges Fail*, addressed the problem. The older 1953 Straus and Bacon study, *Drinking in College*, documented the effects of alcohol use and abuse on campus. But beyond these works, serious research was weak to nonexistent.

Intrigued, I turned to the literature on alcohol and other drug use among young people in general. I found that the most promising education and prevention programs used positive peer pressure to get their message across. Just as negative peer pressure was a factor in alcohol use and abuse, positive peer pressure could be channeled to control it. Armed with this idea, I had many conversations with students and campus officials about how to mobilize students as a positive force for education and prevention. To my surprise, lots of students were interested and eager to join the conversation. This was encouraging.

I thought, Why not organize students to be a voice for moderation and responsibility? Late in the fall of 1975 I called a meeting of students to brainstorm ways of accomplishing that goal. Some twenty-five students showed up. Together, we discussed how to continue their involvement and gain support for our message of moderation. These students didn't want to come across as prohibitionist moral crusaders. That approach had failed across the board. They wanted to do something positive.

We brainstormed. Finally, we decided to become an official student organization called Bacchus—the Roman mythological god of wine and revelry, famous for his debauchery. With a name like Bacchus, no one would mistake us for a temperance group. But we needed an acronym. I suggested calling ourselves "Boost Alcohol Consciousness Concerning the Health of University Students (BACCHUS)." It was a hit.

In the following days, BACCHUS began to attract local media attention and more student interest. A group of college students, concerned about alcohol abuse and promoting a positive message about reducing alcohol abuse problems among their peers—this was unprecedented. It was also newsworthy. Word about BACCHUS spread on campus and across the state.

We had built the foundation for what eventually became America's largest collegiate organization for preventing alcohol abuse. BACCHUS flourished. In fact, it consumed my full-time attention as a graduate student and emerging professional.

Years later, famed author Dr. Stephen R. Covey co-authored a book titled *The 3rd Alternative: Solving Life's Most Difficult Problems*, in which he profiles people from all walks of life who have brought creative solutions, peace, and healing to some of the world's most perplexing problems. Writing about BACCHUS, he said: "Gerardo and his friends set in motion an entirely new approach to helping young people avoid risky behaviors, what is now called the 'peer education' or 'peer support' movement . . . and it works, perhaps better than any other approach out there." (Covey 2011, 188).

## The Wedding and Doctoral Program

Encouraged by BACCHUS's success, I decided to pursue doctoral studies. I hadn't completed my master's requirements, but in December 1975, I applied to the PhD program in counselor education and student personnel administration. I wanted to focus my research on promoting health and preventing alcohol abuse among college students. My statement of professional goals and experiences read, in part: "My professional goals have become more solidified. . . . I am interested in preparing myself for a position of leadership in higher learning. . . . My experiences as a graduate student have consistently led to a greater interest in working with college students."

December 1975 was special for another reason: Marjorie and I got engaged. It wasn't a sudden decision—more like the obvious next step. I never proposed. I didn't go down on my knees. I didn't worry whether she'd agree. I simply told Marjorie that I'd soon finish my master's degree, and we should start planning our wedding. This formalized what we both wanted. In March 1976, I received my master's degree and was admitted to the doctoral program.

On April 10, 1976, we stood inside the fairly new Holy Faith Catholic Church in Gainesville. It was a simple, modern church, led by Father James Flannan Walsh, an Irish priest who had founded the parish in 1972.

My parents, Marjorie's parents, my sister—who, with Marjorie's sister, was a member of the bridal party—and other relatives attended the wedding. Tommy was my best man. Roland came from New Jersey, and Dean Goodale and other friends celebrated with us. It was a beautiful ceremony. Marjorie wore an elegant but simple off-white dress and a rolling twenties-style hat with a lace veil flowing over her shoulders. When she walked up the aisle toward me, I was captivated by her charm and beauty. I knew this woman so well. Yet when I saw her, she took my breath away, just as she takes my breath away to this day.

We had a short, sweet honeymoon—a night and a morning in St. Augustine, a quaint, historic little coastal city in northeast Florida, not far from Gainesville. Founded in 1565 by Spanish Admiral Pedro Menéndez de Avilás, St. Augustine is the oldest continuously occupied European settlement in North America. We didn't have much time to explore St. Augustine's history, however. Right after our honeymoon, we went back to work. To this day, Marjorie reminds me that I owe her a honeymoon.

Back in Gainesville, Marjorie returned to work as a retail manager. Her income supplemented my graduate assistant salary as we built a home together and I pursued my doctoral studies.

The chairman of my doctoral committee was Dr. Harold Riker, a seasoned student affairs administrator and senior faculty member. For many years, he'd been director of the university's division of housing. He was an elderly senior statesman in the field and commanded lots of national and international respect. He was known as a tough doctoral chair and a stickler for technical writing. He covered student papers with corrections and revisions. It was common to submit a draft paper or chapter to Dr. Riker and get it back with more red ink than black. Students feared his red pen.

I completed my doctoral studies in the summer of 1978. On August 26, I again walked across the stage at the University of Florida commencement ceremonies, this time hooded as a newly minted PhD. Again, as with my bachelor's graduation ceremony five years earlier, my parents, my sister, and Marjorie—now my wife and pregnant with our second son—celebrated with me. Dean Goodale, my mentor and member of my doctoral committee, hooded me during

Marjorie preparing for our wedding ceremony.

the ceremonies. Our first son, Justin, born in February 1977, was too young to attend. I was proud, yet humbled, that just a few years earlier, I had no idea what college was about. Yet here I was, receiving the highest credential an academic institution can bestow.

# 8  Professional Transitions

I TOOK A short break to celebrate graduation. Then back to work I went. Student-run BACCHUS chapters were forming on all Florida campuses and in other states. Some of the biggest, most prestigious public and private campuses across the country were expressing interest—the University of Michigan, the University of North Carolina at Chapel Hill, Brown University, Boston College, The Ohio State University, Oregon State University, Indiana University, the University of Maryland, the University of New Mexico, Cornell University, and hundreds of others. I was invited to speak about BACCHUS on college campuses and at state and national conferences, from one end of the country to the other. Some events were well attended, others not; but I never refused an invitation to promote our work.

## The Growth of BACCHUS

We'd begun with a little university funding, and within three years, BACCHUS had blossomed into a statewide, then national program of extraordinary repute. Dean Goodale, himself a figure of good repute, proudly pointed to our campus and state as leaders in confronting a major problem every college campus faced. The message was resonating on every level. On January 30, 1980, BACCHUS was formally chartered as a national not-for-profit corporation under the laws of the State of Delaware.

This vibrant organization needed an infrastructure. A board of trustees—eight national leaders—became our inaugural governing body. I was named president and CEO. BACCHUS bylaws provided for a national advisory council of leaders in such domains as education, business, sports, communications, and government. Indiana Governor Otis R. Bowen, MD, then in his second term, agreed to serve as chair. Governor Bowen was a family physician, former chair of the Education Commission of the States, and chair of the National Governor's Conference. He had received the American Medical Association's Benjamin Rush Award for his leadership in health education and advocacy for preventing alcohol abuse. The council met for the first time in Indianapolis on April 3, 1980.

Governor Bowen chaired the advisory council until 1985, when President Ronald Reagan appointed him secretary of the US Department of Health and Human Services (HHS). Just before his appointment, he'd served as the Lester D. Bibler

At the BACCHUS first general assembly in 1981. I am presenting a plaque to Governor Otis R. Bowen, MD, chairman of the BACCHUS National Advisory Council.

Professor of Family Medicine and director of Undergraduate Family Practice in the Indiana University Department of Family Medicine in Indianapolis.

BACCHUS grew rapidly in five years under the guidance of its advisory council and board of trustees. The November/December 1985 BACCHUS newsletter listed some 240 active chapters in forty-five states and Canada. But the demands of the organization and related travel, along with my responsibilities at the University of Florida, were starting to take a toll on my family life. I now had four kids: Justin, my oldest son, was eight; Jarrett, my second-oldest son, was six; and my youngest son, Ian, was two. My only daughter and youngest child, Julie, was born in June 1985.

Throughout this time Marjorie, the kids, and I continued to make occasional trips to Miami where my parents and my sister, now married, lived together in a single household with two separate living quarters. The demands of my professional life meant we couldn't visit as much as we used to. But over the years, the kids developed a close relationship with their *abuelos*—grandparents—and *tia*—aunt. Every time we visited my parents, just as they had done years earlier for Marjorie and me, my parents made sure the kids got some small gift to take with them.

## Leaving BACCHUS

Early in 1986, I told the BACCHUS board of trustees I planned to resign. I'd led BACCHUS for ten years and was itching to move on. I wanted to pursue my academic career in teaching and research and focus on being full-time faculty. We hadn't solved the college or national drinking problem, but we'd started a national conversation about drinking on campus and student well-being that transformed the way colleges responded to the problem. I was proud of what we'd accomplished. I'd leave at the end of the fiscal year, on September 30. By then, the number of campuses with BACCHUS chapters had risen to 260.

Word got around. *The Chronicle of Higher Education* sent a reporter to Florida and ran a full-page story with the headline, "Alcohol-Education Pioneer Tots Up a Decade of Success" (Ingalls 1986). It read, in part: "Now, some 10 years after its founding here at the University of Florida, Mr. González's brainchild—called BACCHUS after the god of wine ... has become one of the most influential alcohol-education and abuse-prevention programs in the country."

## Unexpected Recognition

When the Honorable T. Terrell Sessums, then chairman of the Florida Board of Regents, read the *Chronicle* article, he sent me a letter that said, in part, "Your dedicated service has helped a large number of young men and women and certainly reflects credit on you and the University of Florida." He copied Charles B. Reed, chancellor of the Florida State University System, and Marshall M. Criser, president of the University of Florida.

I was surprised, honored, and humbled by the many congratulatory notes from colleagues and other state officials. Another came from the esteemed Otis R. Bowen, MD, former BACCHUS chair. He wrote, "For the usual retirement celebration—we would call this a final tribute. But, for you Gerardo, your work will be seen for generations.... All the efforts that you and others have made for BACCHUS will be part of the American way of life." He added, "Knowing how modest you are, I thought that if you heard it from someone else, you would really believe that you have made an extraordinary impact on the lives of young people of this nation. I have enclosed a special message from the White House."

> The message said:
>
> "I understand that for the last ten years you have dedicated yourself to developing a successful alcohol education program for college students. It is comforting to know of your efforts.... Nancy and I are proud of the work you have done to help make a safe and healthy tomorrow for our nation's young people. That's a fine contribution to your adopted homeland."
>
> The signature: "President Ronald Reagan."

THE WHITE HOUSE

WASHINGTON

November 5, 1986

Dear Dr. Gonzalez:

I understand that for the last ten years you have
dedicated yourself to developing a successful alcohol
education program for college students.  It is com-
forting to know of your efforts.  Young people and
their parents across our country can be thankful
that you have worked so hard to educate college
students about alcohol.  I am pleased to know of
the success you and all the students representing
the 250 BACCHUS chapters have had in "Boosting
Alcohol Consciousness Concerning the Health of
University Students."

Nancy and I are proud of the work you have done
to help make a safe and healthy tomorrow for our
nation's young people.  That's a fine contribution
to your adopted homeland.  We join Secretary
Bowen, your friends and colleagues, and especially
the students, in saluting you.  Thank you and God
bless you.

Sincerely,

*Ronald Reagan*

Gerardo Gonzalez, Ph.D.
7624 Southwest 18th Place
Gainesville, Florida  32607

Letter of commendation from President Ronald Reagan.

I sat in my office and read and reread President Reagan's words: "your
adopted homeland." The president of the United States. I was overwhelmed.
The president—the man in the White House—wrote those words. He acknowl-
edged I was an immigrant, a refugee in an adopted homeland. He praised my

contribution. I'd overcome my difficult beginnings, and done something meaningful. Again, I reflected on my parents' sacrifices and their words about the importance of education.

My parents' encouragement, my long-ago conversation with Rafael—all steered me toward education, toward college. President Reagan's words confirmed that for poor people and immigrants like us, education was the key to success. Without a college education, I could never have accomplished what I'd done. I was only thirty-five.

I remembered my middle school humiliation—the vice principal in Miami shouting, "¡*Buena conducta!*—Good conduct!—Behave well!" He was the antithesis of a good teacher. Did he ever think about the damage his kind of discipline caused? He made me believe I wasn't "college material." How would he feel now, knowing I had a desk in a major American university, ran a national program of profound impact, and been praised by the president of the United States for the "fine contribution" I'd made to my adopted homeland? ¡*Buena conducta!*

I looked forward to the next phase of my life and career. I wanted to teach, to inspire other young people to pursue their dreams through education. I couldn't wait to begin a faculty position at a major research university.

## Transitioning to the Faculty

The *Chronicle*'s observation that I wanted to teach in college paved the way. Chancellor Reed congratulated me and asked why I was leaving the University of Florida. After ten years of working with BACCHUS, fundraising, and traveling, I said, I wanted a traditional faculty role in teaching and research. Chancellor Reed invited me to apply for a faculty position in the UF Department of Counselor Education.

It was odd, interviewing with my former professors. I'd known them for years, first as a student, then as a professional staff and affiliate faculty. I'd earned their respect; they valued my accomplishments. My teaching evaluations were good and my research, strong. They were impressed that I'd built an international program, raised funds, and kept it going for ten years. On their recommendation, the dean offered me a full-time position as an associate professor without tenure, beginning in January 1987. In two years, I could apply for tenure and promotion to full professor.

## Making Adjustments

My first year on the faculty was one of the most productive times of my life. I had the smallest office in the department, but so what? I was free from administration! I concentrated on teaching and research. Two years later, the department chair, Dr. Joe Wittmer, stepped down after fifteen years of distinguished service. Many academic institutions drew department chairs from tenured faculty in the department. But the UF College of Education usually conducted national searches. The dean asked the faculty to recommend an interim chair to serve during the search process. The faculty chose me.

Dean David C. Smith knew it wouldn't be an easy sell. He knew my history in administration. I'd come to the college to escape administration. It was 1989 and I'd submitted my dossier for tenure and promotion to full professor. But he pressed his case. The assignment would be short-term.

I was reluctant, but I accepted. The search cast a wide, national net, seeking a strong leader for what was then the nation's top-ranked counselor education department. Three excellent candidates interviewed and met with the faculty. That was good progress. I was eager for the search to end well. I looked forward to returning to the faculty full-time.

At the end of the search: a big surprise. The faculty chose none of the candidates. Instead, in 1990, Dean Smith encouraged me to accept the role of permanent chair. Again, loyalty and commitment to service prevailed. I accepted. But now, I began to wonder. Were these administrative callings my destiny? My readings in Eastern philosophy came back. Maybe administration was bad karma. I'd have to do it in this life or the next!

As department chair, I was the highest-ranking and only Hispanic faculty administrator on campus. One of my first assignments was to co-chair a presidential task force examining the status of African Americans and Hispanics at UF and recommend policies and programs to make the campus more welcoming to minority students. The task force recommended including Hispanics under affirmative action policies and establishing a campus institute for Hispanic and Latino cultures. Both recommendations were accepted and later implemented.

The institute—*La Casita*, a Spanish term for home away from home—became the campus center for advocacy and programs for Hispanic faculty and students. As La Casita grew, I thought about Juan and the other Hispanic students who'd dropped out because of cultural isolation and detachment. I hoped Hispanic faculty, students, and staff would see La Casita as a true symbol of institutional commitment and support, a place where future generations of Latinos could find a sense of community.

## More Bad Karma

I'd chaired the counselor education department for three years. Then the executive associate dean of the College of Education retired. Again, Dean Smith encouraged me to apply for the position. "But I'd come to the college to get away from administration," I said. He persisted. "Consider it. Someday you'll be a great dean—it's in your future."

The same bad karma. Again. It looked like administration was a matter of fate. I'd do it in this life or the next. Period.

After an internal search, I was offered the position. With much trepidation, I accepted, effective July 1, 1993. I was responsible for managing the budget, faculty relations, overseeing the faculty tenure and promotions process, and organizing accreditation, among other things. Through the details of daily administration, I was cutting my teeth on the general challenges of managing a complex organization. Just as I began to feel comfortable in the role, Dean Smith announced his plans to retire at the end of 1994.

Roderick J. McDavis, formerly dean of the College of Education at the University of Arkansas, replaced Dean Smith. He was not new to UF. He'd begun his professorial career as a junior faculty at UF in the counselor education department. In fact, he'd been my first faculty advisor. I'd never forget my first encounter with Dean McDavis.

It's common in many academic institutions to give junior faculty the smallest, least desirable offices in their departments. Dean McDavis was no exception. When he was appointed to the UF faculty, he was assigned a very small office on the fourth floor of Old Norman Hall. This had been a K-12 laboratory school that had been converted to be part of the College of Education. The office was in the furthest corner of the building, an area that had once been the laboratory school's attic. I was a new student and had learned that Dean McDavis was my faculty advisor. So, off I went to his office to introduce myself. Finding his office wasn't easy. First I had to climb several flights of stairs that seemed to lead nowhere. They were concrete, gravel-like stairs, well-worn by decades of student traffic. They led to a narrow hallway on the fourth floor. There, at the end of the hallway, was a corner room that seemed to correspond to the room number for Dean McDavis' office.

I approached the office. The door was open, and I simply walked in. Sitting behind an old desk that looked like a 1950s schoolteacher desk was Dean McDavis. He was a youthful-looking African American man, impeccably dressed. I don't know who was more startled, Dean McDavis or me. He just looked up. For a few seconds, we just looked at each other, without saying a word. Finally, he said, "Can I help you?" I was meeting my advisor for the first time. I was nervous. In a heavily Spanish-accented voice, I mumbled my name. I said I was a new student in the department, and that I had learned he was my advisor. I'm not sure he understood what I said. But he quickly put me at ease with, "Well come in, sit down and relax."

That was the beginning of a long and warm friendship. Dean McDavis was more than an advisor to me—he was a mentor and role model. As an African American man, Dean McDavis understood the plight of minorities at predominantly white institutions in a very deep and personal way. He was a strong advocate for minority concerns and sensitive to my struggles as a Latino man still trying to fit in. He was always quick to offer a supportive word when I needed it most. He went on to become associate dean of the graduate school at the University of Florida and served in that role until his appointment at the University of Arkansas.

When Dean McDavis returned to Florida as dean of the College of Education, I resigned as his executive associate dean. This was the custom—it allowed the dean to choose his own senior staff. But he rejected my resignation, and I remained in the role. As he had been as my advisor, Dean McDavis was more than a supervisor; he was a caring colleague and friend. Our kids played on the same soccer team, and we spent time together at games and tournaments. His wife Deborah and Marjorie also became friends and frequently sat together at soccer games to cheer the team.

I admired Dean McDavis's vision for the college and the energy he brought to his leadership role. He immediately engaged the faculty in a strategic planning process that led to a more focused mission statement and energized a spirit of reform. But not everyone in the college appreciated his style. Some faculty resisted the pace of change. They pushed back. Undeterred, he moved forward with revising the curriculum, increasing access for minority students, and reorganizing the college. Partisans of the status quo especially resented the reorganization.

As executive associate dean, I was expected to implement Dean McDavis's initiatives. We acted as a team. Some appreciated our commitment to innovation. Others swore we were destroying all that was good about the college. We simply wanted to make a positive difference, and I believed in our goals.

Dean McDavis and I often stayed in the office long after business hours. We chatted about all kinds of things—the day's events, future plans, our kids, and so on. Sometimes we put ourselves in the shoes of those used to a university rooted in Southern tradition. They hadn't experienced African Americans and Latinos in leadership roles. We tried to imagine how it felt to be pushed to change by an African American dean and an Hispanic associate dean. We were sympathetic, but that didn't stop us.

Dean McDavis's reputation as a change agent grew, and institutions across the country tried to recruit him for higher-level positions. In 1999, he accepted the post of vice president for academic affairs and provost at Virginia Commonwealth University. After that, he moved on to become president of his alma mater, Ohio University in Athens.

When Dean McDavis left, the provost asked me to serve as interim dean of the college. I was happy to accept the invitation but unsure whether to be a candidate for the dean's position. Several faculty and colleagues across the campus encouraged me, then Dean McDavis nominated me. After thoughtful consideration, I applied for the job.

I had no intentions of applying for dean anywhere else. If offered the position, I'd simply drop "interim" from my title, and keep doing what I was doing. If

University of Florida ceremony honoring College of Education deans (*from left*) Roderick J. McDavis, David C. Smith, me, and Ben F. Nelms, who followed me as interim dean.

I wasn't, it meant I'd served my penance for bad karma. I'd gladly return to being full-time faculty.

But right in the middle of the UF search, I received a call from Indiana University. The School of Education was looking for a dean. The search committee co-chairs Jack Cummings, a professor of educational psychology, and Carlos Ovando, professor of curriculum and instruction, knew I was a candidate at UF. They asked me to consider being a candidate at IU. I had no intentions of pursuing any other position, I said, but appreciated their reaching out. They wouldn't take no for an answer. They said materials about the search were on the way. They'd call again. Perhaps they could change my mind.

I knew the reputation of Indiana University and its School of Education. Over the years, I'd worked with some of the school's most distinguished faculty. Their impact on the field of education was impressive. I admit, I was intrigued by the possibilities. So when Jack and Carlos called again, I agreed to consider IU.

I told Marjorie about my decision. Her reaction: "Where's Indiana?" I called my parents with my news about Indiana. Perhaps moved by memories of our winter in Pittsburgh, my mother simply said, "*Hace mucho frío allí*—It's very cold over there."

# 9 Introduction to Hoosier Culture

Now I faced a dilemma. Two universities had decided I was the only acceptable candidate for dean: the College of Education at the University of Florida, and the School of Education at Indiana University. It would have been easy to stay at UF. I knew it well and had good relationships with the university community. My parents, sister, and even some high school friends lived in Miami, an easy drive from Gainesville. But did I want to retire at the University of Florida, and never experience another institution or community setting?

Indiana University impressed me. The Bloomington campus was beautiful in the fall, winter, and spring, each season with its own distinct and inviting character. The winter wasn't at all like the winter in Pittsburgh. I had actually enjoyed walking on campus in the snow.

I also loved IU for the civility of peoples' interactions and the quality of their relationships. Relationships have always been important to me. I felt there must be something very special about a university community where, even in the hustle and bustle of a high-intensity dean's search, you could develop deep relationships.

IU's values and traditions appealed to me. The university's former beloved president and chancellor Herman B Wells made IU prominent as a research university, nationally and internationally. He was a model of the important role leaders can play in creating an institutional culture that protects fundamental shared values that serve generations of faculty, students, and society. I was especially taken by Wells's outspoken support for academic freedom and its role in empowering faculty to do research without outside interference. I was impressed by his legendary defense of sex researcher Alfred Kinsey when public discussion of human sexuality was taboo. IU history professor James H. Capshew said, "Wells doggedly took on Alfred Kinsey's detractors, giving the university an enviable reputation as a bastion of free inquiry." (Capshew, n.d.)

Then there was my own belief in change. I have always been fond of the teachings of the Greek philosopher Heraclitus of Ephesus. He expressed his belief in the universal nature of change through his well-known phrase, "You can't step twice in the same river." I take this to mean that if you focus your life and work on doing the very best you can in the present, change, by its very nature, will move you to the next phase of your existence. Somehow going to Indiana just felt like the right thing to do.

# CHALKBOARD

Indiana University School of Education Alumni Association          Fall/Winter 2000

## Gerardo Gonzalez
### Education's Eighth Dean

*Chalkboard*, the Indiana University School of Education alumni magazine, announces my appointment as the school's eighth dean.

## A Difficult Choice

But on a personal level, deciding to leave Florida was tough. My moving to Indiana would be a major change for my family. It would be especially hard for my children, oldest to youngest. Justin was in Miami trying to start a business. Jarrett was a student at UF. My third son Ian and my daughter Julie were entering their junior and sophomore years in high school. The move would be especially hard for them—we'd never been apart. As Marjorie and I said goodbye to Jarrett, he looked at me rather sadly and said, "I feel like somehow my life is going to change forever, but you'll do great. I'll come visit as soon as you settle in." My parents would not have left Cuba without the support of their families. I, too, needed my family's support to uproot. I knew my parents were concerned about my moving so far away. My parents had been my inspiration. Now my family was my support.

## A Successful First Year

I accepted IU's offer and settled into my office in the W. W. Wright Education Building. Right away I began to meet people and get to know the faculty, staff, students, and administration I'd be working with. I met with alumni groups, donors, and community and state leaders. I received a warm welcome from State Senator Vi Simpson, a highly respected state leader who represented IU's district. Like me, she saw education as the "great equalizer" in a democratic society. She invited me to call on her if I ever needed her assistance. Given the politics I'd experienced in Florida, where politicians typically called on academics only when they had a special project to push or some favor to ask, this was extraordinary.

I've always felt that culture is key in creating environments that foster positive interaction and change. In all these meetings, I again felt the Hoosier warmth and civility that had drawn me here. The more I learned about what it meant to be a Hoosier, the more I liked it. This culture fit my personality and style of leadership. I'd made the right decision.

In my first year as dean, I worked with the faculty, staff, and students to develop a strategic plan. Our mission statement captured the essence of the twenty-first-century global community in which the school and its faculty would function, working to "improve teaching, learning, and human development in a global, diverse, rapidly changing, and increasingly technological society." Our strategic goals—high-quality teacher preparation, enhanced doctoral education and research, leadership in technology, increased engagement with public schools, and greater diversity among faculty and students—were designed to "provide a framework for making future investments to increase and assess the school's quality and productivity." The mission statement and goals were widely distributed to the campus as part of my *First Annual Report to Faculty*.

Then IU president Myles Brand congratulated me, my colleagues, and the students on the report's range and depth of activity. Later that year, Chancellor Gros Louis wrote, "I have been amazed at how quickly and correctly you have understood the unique culture of Bloomington." And Leo Fay, a respected senior faculty member in the School of Education, said of my first year as dean, "You rate among the very top ... a very promising sign for the future of the school."

But sometimes fate—destiny, karma, kismet—call it what you will—intervenes and skittles you like a heavy ball in a bowling alley.

## The Winds of Change

The once-civil public discourse on education changed when Mitch Daniels was elected Indiana governor in 2004. The theme of his first State of the State Address, delivered to the General Assembly on January 18, 2005, was that everything in state government was broken and needed to be fixed. He called for a freeze in state funding for K-12 and higher education and changes in the public school funding formula. He urged the spread of charter schools, publicly funded schools run independently by non-profit boards outside the traditional public school system. Of the state government, Daniels said that "every garden needs weeding every 16 years or so."

Daniels claimed more than once that Indiana's educational results lagged behind other states. He was incorrect. In fact, high school graduation rates in Indiana were among the country's highest. Underrepresented or minority students were performing well compared to those in other states. True to his administration's combative approach, Daniels concluded his remarks with quotes from wartime correspondent Edward R. Murrow and General Douglas MacArthur. I was worried about this change in discourse, but my focus was on the school—strengthening partnerships with schools and communities, recruiting more underrepresented faculty and students, and otherwise implementing our strategic plan—not on fighting the State's reform initiatives.

But in 2008, when Daniels was elected to a second term, I could no longer stay out of state politics. Dr. Tony Bennett became state superintendent of public instruction. He reminded me of the Shenandoah Middle School vice principal who'd made my life miserable in Miami. Bennett was a crew-cut former coach who wore straight-legged pants and button-down shirts. He was dictatorial and abrasive to anyone who disagreed with him. But we were cordial, and I offered the school's help in implementing his agenda. I made a special effort to meet with Dr. Bennett early in his tenure as state superintendent and invited him to participate on an annual panel the school offered every fall for alumni in Indianapolis. He agreed.

## REPA: A Moral Challenge

In the summer of 2009, shortly after my meeting with Dr. Bennett, we were on the way to a planned family summer vacation at Myrtle Beach, South Carolina. I happened to check my cell phone at the airport. The news was disturbing. A political initiative, headed by Dr. Bennett, was underway that would launch one of the defining issues of my years as dean. On my phone were multiple voice messages and emails from reporters who wanted my opinion on Bennett's proposal. Andy Gammill, the education reporter for *The Indianapolis Star*, explained the proposal and the response by the Indiana Professional Standards Board (IPSB).

In our earlier meeting, Bennett had failed to mention this proposal. It called for major changes in education in the state. The Rules for Educator Preparation and Accountability (REPA) claimed we needed new ways to prepare and license educators. It said teachers needed more knowledge in the subject they taught and should major in a discipline instead of in education. It also called for greater flexibility in teacher licensing to improve the quality of teachers. These changes were extremely complex and highly controversial. All state teacher preparation standards and licensing had to be approved by the IPSB, but the board received the REPA proposal only a few days before its July 2009 meeting, when it was expected to vote. Many state educators had publicly expressed dismay about a proposal they'd never heard of.

That same evening, then IU Vice President for Academic Affairs and Provost Karen Hanson called to say that IU's president was concerned about the politics surrounding REPA and I needed to tread carefully. I understood those concerns, but worried that some of REPA's major provisions threatened to damage K-12 education and teacher preparation and put at risk the integrity of the university curriculum. REPA would cause a major break with tradition. The State dictating the content and structure of the curriculum at independent colleges and public universities would be an affront to the principle of academic freedom. REPA made some of the most sweeping proposals for changing teacher licensure in the state, but the deans of education hadn't heard about it until the day before the IPSB meeting.

Superintendent Bennett then launched a media tour to promote REPA. A September 2009 Associated Press story said that schools of education required students who majored in math education to take only a few math classes. In an editorial, I pointed to the errors in these statements: "Let's be very clear: that's not true." But a Bennett spokesperson persisted: under REPA, teachers would gain more content knowledge. Clearly, the superintendent's office wasn't interested in facts, but in political spectacle promoting an ill-informed education reform agenda. Some university presidents urged their education deans not to testify or speak out against REPA for fear of state retribution. IU's president, Michael McRobbie, too, was under a lot of political pressure. But consistent with IU's traditions of academic freedom, he never asked me not to speak out on the merits of the proposal. That was important to me.

## Outspoken Opposition

In Florida, I'd opposed Jeb Bush's "One Florida" initiative (Klein and Kassab 2000). This initiative abolished affirmative action in recruiting faculty and students to the state's public universities. Not only that, but it was put into effect by executive order, without input from faculty, students, or community leaders. One Florida was my first taste of the kind of threat state control could pose to higher education and to minorities. REPA seemed to mount an even more serious affront to the principles of academic freedom and democratic culture.

I'd lived through the Castro regime, with its muffling of dissidents and its stifling of the press. I vividly remembered our fear of government control—the watchdog committees that changed neighborhoods into nests of suspicion, the surveillance that dogged my father as he listened to his radio. Private and religious schools, cast as enemies of the state, were nationalized. My parents had fled a country whose government took control of their children's education, their schools, and their freedom of expression. As a nation and a culture, we had been bullied. I had been bullied as a kid, just for being part of a family that didn't support the new system. I would not be bullied again.

To not speak out against REPA would have been akin to sanctioning a return to the McCarthy era, when professors had to take an oath of loyalty to save their jobs (Schrecker 1999). That wasn't the standard Wells set for Indiana University. Thanks to his historic support of faculty's right to work free of outside interference, IU earned a reputation as a global public research university. IU's flagship campus at Bloomington is recognized for innovation and creativity—hallmarks of academic freedom and integrity.

Under Wells's leadership, IU had developed the institutional culture that drew me to Indiana. My responsibility as dean was to serve as steward and promoter of the very culture that REPA now challenged. For me, opposing REPA was a matter of principle and a way of protecting IU's culture.

In late October and early November, the Indiana Department of Education held three public hearings on REPA. I became the face of REPA opposition. The superintendent's office, governor staff, legislators, and other officials pressured me to back off. But my message was getting through. More than 200 people showed up at the IU alumni program that Bennett and I had discussed. Most opposed REPA. Reporters from National Public Radio and other media covered the event and challenged the superintendent's assertions. Bennett was furious with me. The next day, he reportedly said to his staff, "He set me up."

I had not set him up. The alumni program had been planned and announced before I had ever heard of REPA. The real problem was that I was exposing the faulty premises behind Bennett's proposals. The opposition to REPA grew far and wide. It was the subject of countless articles, op-ed pieces, public testimony, and multiple public hearings.

Opposition to REPA spread among deans of education, media, alumni, parents, students, and the community. Largely as a result of that public exposure and debate, the version of REPA that Governor Daniels signed into law in March 2010 was almost a shadow of Bennett's original concept. The final proposal incorporated most of the adjustments requested by state schools of education and other teacher preparation organizations. I'm proud to say I was largely responsible for that.

The REPA controversy consumed an inordinate amount of my time. But if I hadn't stuck my neck out as the voice of opposition, Dr. Bennett's drive to undermine teacher preparation would have spread nationally. This sudden, unwarranted fight against the political machine did two things. It raised a national voice of opposition to some popular but wrongheaded education policy ideas. And it reminded me of what the United States had done for me, and which was now under threat: prepare caring and effective educators on whom young people could depend in their quest to become contributing citizens.

You know you're on the side of the angels when your opponents' arguments have no substance. I knew I'd done the right thing for education at IU, in the state, and in the nation. An informed public had spoken out.

As many feared, however, opposing powerful political figures had consequences. My standard second five-year dean's review took place during the REPA debate. The review committee received an unsigned statement from the Indiana Department of Education (IDOE) that read, in part, "Dean González is the 'best' example of what needs to change in Indiana higher education leadership in order for more progressive ideas to be fairly considered [and] openly discussed."

Did it bother me that the letter called me the worst example of an educator?

Quite the opposite. The unsigned letter did more than attack me; it assaulted peoples' rights to speak freely. As long as I was responsible for educating our future teachers and school administrators, I would defend faculty against threats to academic values, support their right to determine their curricula, and to prepare future teachers as role models and inspirational leaders. I'd fight for the integrity of the institution and the moral principles that underlie a democratic society and an open academic culture.

## Opening Doors for Others

During my political struggles as dean, memories of my previous leadership roles and encounters I'd had with minority and poor students flooded back. They reminded me of the transformative power of education and why it is so important to defend the right to a quality education for all students, especially those who'd been denied that. One particularly memorable encounter involved a project funded while I was chairman of counselor education at Florida. This project supported educational, cultural, and technical interchange between the United States and Latin America, the Caribbean, and Canada. It tested a drug education curriculum in five public and five private middle schools in La Paz, Bolivia (González and Kaune Moreno 1995). In one of the discussions I led with students, a young lady sat crying. I reached out to her and asked if she was all right. "*Sí, señor, estoy bien*—Yes, sir, I'm fine," she said. I asked, "*¿Y por qué lloras?*—Why do you cry?" Her words resonate to this day. She said, "*Ay señor, no ves que soy india. Mire que india soy. Yo nunca podre expresarme con otros como usted nos enseñó*—Ay señor, can't you see I'm Indian. Look how Indian I am. I will never be able to express myself to others the way you have taught us." Then, pointing to her facial features, she said, "*Me duele mucho saber que hay mejor manera de ser y no puedo serlo por quien soy yo*—It pains me to know there's a better way to be and I could never realize it because of who I am."

Her words brought back the humiliation and prejudice I'd experienced as a kid in the United States. Just like this beautiful girl, I was picked on because I was different. Her words reminded me that many of the great inequalities in this world are related to the circumstances of our birth, many of which we can't control: race, customs, language, skin color, and physical features. I empathized with her feeling of helplessness. I felt her pain.

I had another encounter in Managua, Nicaragua, that was just as painful. I was there to investigate expanding educational opportunities. A young boy of about eleven or twelve—the age at which I'd left my native Cuba—was selling chickens on the street. I asked him, "*¿Por qué no estas en la escuela?*—Why aren't you in school?" He simply looked at me and said, "*Señor, tengo que comer*—Sir, I have to eat." There was nothing I could say to him. But I thought, If not for the grace of education, that boy could be me.

Another experience occurred closer to home. A high school in Frankfort, Indiana, was participating in an IU federally funded research project to train teachers to teach English using subject-area instruction. Frankfort is a rural community north of Indianapolis, whose poultry processing plants drew a growing Hispanic and Latino immigrant population. The lead faculty on the research, Faridah Pawan, a native of Malaysia and an immigrant herself, invited me to see the project at work.

The school held a special assembly for Hispanic and Latino students, where I shared my immigrant's story of my struggles to learn the language in American schools. The students listened intently. I stressed the importance of studying hard and preparing for college. As I spoke, I noticed a student in the second row had tears in her eyes. Several students stayed around to talk after my presentation. The girl who had been crying remained in her seat. When the others left, I approached her and asked the same question I'd asked the lovely young lady in Bolivia: "*¿Que pasá, por qué lloras?*—What's the matter, why are you crying?"

She said, "I am crying because everything you said is true." She continued, "I want to go to college, and I know it's important, but I can't." I asked her why. She replied, "Because I'm undocumented. I'm afraid that if I apply to college immigration will come to take my parents away."

I was heartbroken. I didn't know what to say; after all, this was happening in America's heartland, not some developing country thousands of miles away. I knew that the US Constitution guarantees an education to undocumented children regardless of immigration status. But nothing I could say would have alleviated that girl's fears of losing her parents because of something she might do. It was hard to leave that school, knowing a motivated and talented student would be denied an education because her parents came to the United States illegally, simply because they wanted their children to have a better life.

Conversations with my parents about why they left Cuba deepened my understanding of the sacrifices that families, especially immigrant families, make for their children. My children are educated and successful because of their grandparents' sacrifices. The blessings of education in a free society will continue for generations to come. No children should be denied an education because their parents sought a better life for them.

My work supporting the underserved and minorities was recognized early and often during my career at IU. In 2003, the IU Latino Faculty and Staff Council gave me its annual service award for my efforts on behalf of Hispanic students. In 2008, Miami Dade, which gave me my start in college, inducted me into its Alumni Hall of Fame. I stood proudly with my mother, my father, and two of my sons at ceremonies that honored some of Miami Dade's greatest alumni, including such notable Cubans as playwright and Pulitzer Prize winner Nilo Cruz, and Emilio Estefan, formerly of the Miami Sound Machine.

In 2012, *Hispanic Business* magazine presented me with its Special Achievement Award as one of the "50 Most Influential Hispanics" in the United States. Honorees come from business, government, executive leadership, and entrepreneurship. I was one of four education leaders. And in 2015, the IU Latino Faculty and Staff Council presented me with its inaugural Outstanding Achievement Award.

These awards touched me deeply. They meant I'd balanced my identities as a Cuban refugee and American, and through the power of education had become a leader. I'd given back to those who, like me, struggled with issues of immigration and adaptation to an all-too-often hostile world.

## Telling My Own Story

In my childhood family, telling stories about the challenges and struggles and successes of our relatives were ways of describing our family culture and values. These stories reflected the importance of family itself, of relationships. The

Telling my story to faculty and students at Indiana University.

importance of hard work, of never giving up. The importance of treating every-one with dignity. Stories were part of our family tradition.

Throughout my career, people have asked me time and time again to tell my own story—the poor immigrant boy who spoke no English, coming to the United States and making a difference in the lives of others and in the nation. It's a story about the transformative power of education, one I'm always proud to share.

Of all the speeches and lectures I've given as dean and educator, those that audiences remember most touch an emotional chord. They help people relate to me and each other on a personal level. Facts and figures have their place, but nothing conveys a message like a story.

Telling my story is a way to encourage others—particularly those with lim-ited educational opportunities—to consider college. I've been proud to be the commencement speaker twice at Bloomington's Ivy Tech Community College. The second time, in 2012, on Chancellor John Whikehart's invitation, I spoke about my high school experience. I described how it felt to be marginalized in the Dade County K-12 school system. It wasn't prepared for English language learn-ers like me, so I was either humiliated or ignored. I didn't care about academics— I just wanted to get by and get out. Spending half-days in a school co-op program, then working in a men's clothing store was paradise. I loved fashion and dreamed of owning my own boutique. But when the recession in the early seventies hit, the store closed. There went my dreams. What next?

This story is also about the power of relationships. Thanks to a trusted friend, I took a bold step. Without his encouragement, I never, ever would have considered college. This is also a story about being open to taking risks. No one had ever talked to me about college—I didn't know how to go about it. But I took some risks and used the resources around me to learn about how to succeed in college. I literally learned about college while in college. Then came the big discovery. I told the class at Ivy Tech, "I quickly realized I wanted to be a lifelong learner." I told them, "The right people at the right times have helped me climb from being that 'invisible' refugee student ... to a highly visible leader among schools of education deans in the United States."

Ivy Tech presented me with an Honorary Associate of Science Degree for College and Community Service. Chancellor Whikehart called me a model for Ivy Tech students to follow. He said I had helped create more pathways for Ivy Tech students by "shepherding Ivy Tech's system-wide education degree articulation with IU" (Indiana University Bloomington 2012).

Ivy Tech reminded me of the institution that long ago had opened doors for me. I was honored to give back. In my heart, I know that graduating class held other unlikely heroes, perhaps even recent refugees. They will make a difference in their own and others' lives because of educational opportunities like mine.

## Today's Challenges: A Matter of Values

Underlying the challenges we face today in education and immigration are questions of values. I worry that US education today is focused on things we can measure—standardized test scores—instead of authentic and deep learning, human development, equal opportunity, social justice, and respect for differences. These core values are foundational to a democracy, and education is key to sustaining them. Indiana's political squabbling and infighting on education policy show that it's easier to destroy a culture built on civil discourse and compromise than it is to re-create one (Krull 2014).

Our nation is now in danger of making the same mistakes over immigration policy as Indiana has made over education. The plight of Hispanic and Latino immigrants is one of our nation's greatest tragedies. Latinos are desperate for opportunities to work, pursue education, and qualify for citizenship. We forget how important it is to welcome those who want to work hard and fit in. Does it matter that they came illegally, in desperation? In an ideal world, a country's borders are secured. But it's impossible to round up and deport the nation's more than eleven million undocumented people. We need to open doors for those who will remain, especially children.

For many years, the US Congress tried but failed to pass various versions of the DREAM Act—Development, Relief and Education for Alien Minors—designed to protect from deportation young immigrants brought to the country illegally by their parents. Frustrated by Congress's failures, in 2012 then president Barack Obama signed an executive order creating the Deferred Action for Childhood Arrivals (DACA) program. DACA allowed illegal immigrants who entered the country as minors, had not committed serious crimes, and met certain other conditions to receive a renewable two-year permit deferring them from deportation and making them eligible for work permits. By 2017, nearly 800,000 so-called "Dreamers" had signed-up for the program. Many states also allowed Dreamers to receive driver's licenses and in-state tuition at public colleges. But on September 5, 2017, President Donald Trump ordered an end to the program and gave Congress a six-month deadline to pass legislation to come up with a replacement.

The order created panic among Dreamers, many of whom feared they would lose their jobs, have to drop out of school, and possibly be deported from the only country they really knew. Many critics, including Democratic and Republican legislators, business leaders, educators, and others, called President Trump's actions "heartless" and "cruel." I was reminded of President Reagan's letter to me and pained by the possibility that in the future no American president would be able to write a Dreamer commending him or her for their "fine contribution to your adopted homeland."

All Dreamers, the vast majority of whom are Latinos and came to this country at an even younger age than I did, should be allowed to pursue the American Dream. Making sure those kids have opportunities is a matter of national survival. If we create conditions that systematically deny opportunity to any given class of people, we position ourselves for the demise of liberty. As a Cuban refugee, I know we can't take our liberty for granted.

Immigration and education are about honoring the rights and the dignity of the individual, regardless of class or station. Chancellor Wells was a common man who never lost touch with the people he served. He established the traditions that make Indiana University "the people's university."

As dean, I translated my experiences as a refugee, immigrant, and new citizen in a democratic society into action to sustain the traditions Wells had championed, prepare exceptional teachers and leaders who expand opportunities for all young people, and confront inequality. Over time, I saw that my understanding the culture and traditions of Indiana University was key to my success as one of the longest-serving deans at the institution. The university attracts faculty and students from every corner of the world because of the reputation and traditions Chancellor Wells helped establish. I had not only survived as an academic leader in that environment—I had thrived.

## Next Steps

When I retired from the deanship on June 30, 2015, after fifteen years of service, President McRobbie presented me with the President's Medal, the highest honor an IU president can bestow for excellence in service, achievement, and leadership.

And maybe I still have some administrative karma to work through. After the thaw in US–Cuban relations, President McRobbie asked me to serve as special advisor to the university's Office of International Affairs on Cuba. This would be a trailblazing role, not just for the university, but for me. I was entering an unfamiliar landscape—educational ambassador—and launching another adventure in which I would do my best.

# 10 Give the Thaw a Chance

Like the rest of the world, I was surprised when, on December 17, 2014, Presidents Barack Obama and Raúl Castro simultaneously announced that the United States and Cuba were reestablishing diplomatic ties. Less than a year later, on July 20, 2015, the American flag flew at the American embassy in Havana for the first time in fifty-four years. In March 2016, President Obama became the first sitting US president to visit Cuba since 1928, when President Calvin Coolidge entered the Havana Harbor aboard the USS *Texas* battleship. Thus began the thaw in more than a half-century of frozen relations.

After the 2014 announcements, the local media asked how I felt about the thaw. Many assumed that because my family had suffered under the revolution, I'd be against the policy. That was not the case. The Indiana University Alumni Association (IUAA) alumni people-to-people visit in 2012 made it clear that fifty years of government hostility couldn't break the personal and cultural bonds between Cubans and Americans. In an opinion column for the *Huffington Post* following the announced thaw, I said, "Clearly, Cold War tactics have not worked in Cuba. Let's give the thaw a chance" (González 2015).

Imagine how I felt, then, as IU's first Cuban American dean, when IU President Michael McRobbie asked me to serve as ambassador for Indiana University to foster engagement with Cuban institutions. A former Cuban refugee, I would now represent Indiana University to forge bonds between educators in Cuba and Indiana. President McRobbie continued to build on Chancellor Wells's contributions to advancing IU as an international university. As special advisor to the IU Office of International Affairs on Cuba Initiatives, I had the opportunity to expand that effort in my own homeland.

## The Official Visit

My role as IU ambassador to Cuba started well. In early June 2015, the Institute of International Education (IIE) announced that Indiana University was one of twelve American universities chosen to take part in an IIE International Academic Partnership Program (IAPP). In light of the warming diplomatic relations, the IAPP goal was to reengage the United States and Cuba in higher education initiatives. Each university would develop a strategic plan for working with Cuban colleges and universities.

We conducted a study tour to learn about Cuba's system of higher education, identify potential partners, and begin to form professional relationships with Cuban counterparts. I led the IU delegation—my first visit to Cuba as an official representative of Indiana University.

I knew it wouldn't be easy to work with Cuban counterparts on such academic collaborations as research, study-abroad, and student exchanges. Getting past ideological differences always requires understanding and respect for others' perspectives and ways of doing things. But more than a half-century of isolation and conflict between the United States and Cuba made that a special challenge. It was a challenge I was willing to undertake because I also felt that the thaw would help bring our two countries closer together and accelerate social, educational, and economic exchanges with Cuba of a kind unthinkable just a few years ago.

## The Itinerary

Coincidentally, I received the IIE study tour itinerary just as the then US secretary of state John Kerry, who had presided over the raising of the American flag ceremony at the newly reopened US Embassy in Havana, delivered the keynote address at the dedication of IU's new School of Global and International Studies. Our packed schedule included visits with senior government officials from the Cuban Ministry of Higher Education; administrators from some of Cuba's leading institutions of higher education; a visit to the Instituto Superior de Arte, the nation's premier institute of art; and stops at some standard cultural and revolutionary historical sites. It also included visits to the Havana residences of Hermán Portocarero, ambassador of the European Union, and Ambassador Jeffrey DeLaurentis, the then US chief of mission.

We were the first high-level delegation of American universities to visit the island since the reopening of diplomatic relations. IIE President and CEO Allan E. Goodman led the delegation, which included members of the organization's IAPP advisory board and some thirty university representatives.

In an IIE news release issued before the visit, President Goodman said, "In our face-to-face meetings with Cuban educators, we have found that the desire to develop partnerships with US colleges and universities is strong." He continued, "The reestablishment of relations between the United States and Cuba paves the way for student and faculty exchange in both directions and allows for joint research that will benefit both of our societies and the world we share."

I agreed with President Goodman. I was fortunate to represent my university on this groundbreaking initiative. But I soon realized that separating the official role from the personal would be harder than I thought.

## Back in Havana

It had been three years since my first visit to Cuba. The thaw had been announced to everyone's surprise. Diplomatic relations had been reestablished. Private business and other market-driven initiatives were growing. I wanted to know how the thaw affected the economy and the mentality of those who'd formerly lived in virtual isolation from the rest of the world.

The short flight from Miami took less than forty-five minutes, but we might as well have landed lightyears away. At the José Martí International Airport in Havana, our Cuban tour guide, Nadia Reyes Castillo, greeted us, and our luggage was whisked off to a large, blue-and-white Amistur bus. Nadia was an intense, dark-skinned, self-identified *mulata*—mixed race—woman who spoke hurried but very good English. I didn't quite get her name, and asked her to repeat it. She said with emphasis, "Nadia, like Nadia Comăneci." She took us on a walking tour of Old Havana, where I noticed that renovation of tourist areas had kept pace since my visit in 2012. We checked in at the upscale Meliã Cohiba hotel, which was built and operated under a partnership between the Spanish and Cuban governments. By Cuban standards, it was comfortable and quite luxurious, but small problems like water leaks in the bathrooms and slow elevators were familiar from my earlier trip.

As was the case during my original visit, there were the hundreds of 1950s-style American cars driving through the streets of Havana. Many of the cars, coughing their smoky exhausts, had been left behind by Cuban emigrants who headed for the United States after the revolution. At the airport, Cuban customs officials had made the owners surrender their keys. The government then distributed the cars to supporters of the revolution as rewards for such things as meeting production quotas or loyalty to the government. Under Raúl Castro's privatization policies, owners can now sell the cars. Many had makeshift *Se Vende*—For Sale—signs on them.

That evening, we walked to dinner at the private Arte Chef restaurant, where the owners greeted us with the customary welcome drink. Among the guests were José Raul Viera Linares, a retired government official, and his wife, Maria Cecilia Bermúdez. When he learned I was from Placetas, Mr. Viera Linares proudly said he had been in charge of nationalizing the Central Zaza sugar mill in Placetas. Central Zaza, Central San José, and Central Fidencia, where my grandfather had worked as a *templero* before the revolution, formed the major local source of employment. I was shocked, but careful not to overreact. I didn't want him to know that my family was among the many whose lives were adversely affected when the government nationalized private property.

I flashed back to my father's story of finding my grandfather in the outhouse with a rope around his neck, desperate, and ready to jump because he could not find work. The Central Fidencia had literally saved his life. I wanted to ask Mr. Viera Linares whether he understood how his actions had affected the hundreds

Old American cars cruising the streets of Havana. Photo courtesy of Doug Kutz.

if not thousands of workers who depended on those sugar mills in Placetas. But I was a member of an academic delegation, so kept my counsel. Such irony.

After dinner we attended a special performance of the *Opera de la Calle*—Street Opera, a nontraditional opera and dance company organized by Maestro Ulises Aquino Guerra, with local talent recruited from the streets of Havana (Canada: Immigration and Refugee Board of Canada 2014). The performers ranged from late teens to middle age. They were talented and dedicated to their art and what it stood for. Afterward, at a private reception, we met with the cast and some special guests. I talked with two members of the cast—a young man in his twenties and a forty-something woman—who expressed doubt about the new post-thaw economic and liberalized social policies. The young man rolled his eyes and kept quiet, but the woman voiced that she doubted she'd see direct benefits in her lifetime. She said, "Perhaps my children or grandchildren, but it's too late for people like me. I don't expect to see the benefits."

The pessimism expressed during these early exchanges in Havana surprised me.

## A Renewed Partnership

Víctor Fowler Calzada, an Afro-Cuban essayist and poet who lectured at Indiana University in February 2015, spoke of the potential for post-thaw Cuba. Considered one of the most important authors of the first generation of writers born in Revolutionary Cuba, he said that Cubans refer to December 17, when the thaw was announced, as "17D." What would be the difference between Cuba before December 17, and after? The biggest obstacle to realizing a better Cuba, said Fowler, is people's reluctance to ask questions. He said, "We have to learn how to ask questions."

Before President Obama's visit to Cuba, Fowler (2016) posed some questions to the Cuban people, including: *"¿Qué piensan de esta visita? ¿Qué esperan de este contacto? ¿Qué quisieran que ocurra más allá? ¿Qué les disgusta y qué desean cambiar de este mundo en el que viven? ¿Qué quieren, del lado opuesto, conservar?*—What do you think about this visit? What do you expect from this contact? What would you like to see happen in the future? What concerns do you have and what would you like to change about this world in which you live? On the other hand, what would you like to conserve?"

Against this backdrop, I was in Cuba to establish new educational partnerships and academic exchanges and discuss questions like those Fowler had asked. We held meetings at the University of Havana, the University of Medical Sciences, and other institutions in Havana.

Next on our agenda was The Universidad Central "Martha Abreu" de Las Villas (UCLV), known in Cuba as Universidad Central. UCLV is located in Santa Clara, the capital city of the province of Villa Clara. Santa Clara, where fifty-five years earlier my father learned his auto repair shop was being nationalized, is only twenty-one miles from my hometown of Placetas. Connecting the two cities is Cuba's Carretera Central, a beautiful stretch of road that winds through mountains and valleys in the lush central Cuban countryside. Our family often traveled that road to visit relatives or enjoy the area's natural sites.

I'd heard and read a lot about UCLV but never visited. I looked forward to visiting the campus and meeting those I'd corresponded with. Everything suggested IU and UCLV would be good institutional partners. But I wondered what it would feel like to visit Santa Clara for the first time since leaving the island as a refugee. I had so many memories, so many emotional ties to Santa Clara. Unlike other businessmen or academics going to the "forbidden" island for the first time, I was returning to the land of my birth. My last memory of Santa Clara was seeing the royal palm trees cruising past the car window as my family headed to the city to say goodbye to relatives before we left Cuba.

Santa Clara held many painful memories of loss, dislocation, and betrayal. For my parents, it was a Communist-governed land they didn't trust. I wondered how I would be received by those who'd lived under Communism and who more

My family with cousin Nelsida Soto (*first from left*) at the Topes de Collantes mountain observatory, Las Villas, circa 1960.

than a half-century ago had cut off my father's ability to conduct his business simply because he didn't want to join a cooperative. So many mixed emotions. I was excited and apprehensive, eager to see places I remembered, and others I'd only heard about. What would I uncover?

As we approached Santa Clara, I was enchanted by the beautiful rural countryside, royal palms everywhere. We passed old tobacco barns made of *guano*—palm leaves strung together to protect against the elements—like the one I had played in with my cousins. We saw small pastel-colored wood-and-concrete houses with red tile or tin roofs and small porches; old, abandoned tractors and other farm equipment; unkempt, overgrown lawns; and clotheslines loaded with items drying in the hot sun. Traveling along the narrow streets and dirt roads at the city outskirts were horse-drawn carts, people on horseback, bicycle taxis, old trucks, and an occasional fifties-era American car. This was the Cuba I remembered.

## A Visit to UCLV

Nadia's "*Ya llegamos*—We've arrived" pulled me from my trance. A large blue sign read, in black letters, "Universidad Central 'Marta Abreu' de Las Villas." "UCLV" stood in a faded pastel backdrop. We passed other blue signs typical of college campuses, identifying academic buildings and specialties—Humanities, Social Sciences, Law, Psychology, and Historical Salon. Red-and-white buildings dotted the campus.

At the biotechnology institute building, a receiving line of university and city officials awaited us, including the UCLV rector, Dr. Andrés Castro Alegría; the UCLV director of international relations, Dr. Alina Montero Torres; the director of international relations for the province of Villa Clara, Mr. Reday René Armas; and the Cuban Institute for Friendship with the Peoples (ICAP) delegate for Villa Clara, Ms. Iris Maura Menéndez Pérez. As I shook hands with each one, Reday René Armas leaned over, looked into my eyes, and said, "*Hemos estado leyendo mucho sobre usted*—We've been reading a lot about you."

At first I was taken aback. Why would they have read about me and not the other delegates? All had distinguished academic careers and held important university positions. Then it dawned on me. I was a special case. I was a Cuban American who had left as an exiled refugee, returning to my native land. Given the history of tensions between the United States and Cuba, and between Cubans on the island and the Cuban American community in the United States, I understood. They didn't know me and probably mistrusted my intentions.

But my intentions were good. I planned to look past ideological differences and sociopolitical orientation and explore a new institutional partnership to improve the lives of Cuban and American students through education and research. I was honored to present Rector Castro Alegría with the delegation's honoraria—a symbol of friendship between the US and Cuban universities. In my remarks to the rector and his colleagues, I tried to convey the pride and emotion of standing in my former province, so close to Placetas. I said, "*Como Villareño y Placeteño*—A person from the province of Villa Clara and a citizen of Placetas—*estoy especialmente orgulloso de representar a la delegación y presentar regalos de cada una de nuestras universidades*—I am especially proud to represent the delegation and present gifts from each of our universities." My using "Villareño" and "Placeteño" signified that I had returned to my homeland. For me, this was so much more than an academic delegation visiting a university. It was a homecoming. My hosts' faces told me they were moved.

As we left UCLV, I reminded Alina, the university's director of international relations, that I planned to return to Santa Clara after the IIE tour to follow up on our partnership discussions. Upon my return, I met with Alina to work on the IU partnership agreement. We identified areas of special interest for collaboration, including study-abroad opportunities for American students, training in teaching English as a second language for teachers and professors, Spanish language and cultural studies in Cuba, and other opportunities for exchanges and research. We agreed that UCLV would draft a general agreement to reflect our discussions and send it to me for review by IU faculty and international program officials. An IU faculty committee reviewed and approved the draft, which was then recommended to President McRobbie for his signature. Almost a year after my first visit to UCLV, this became the first post-thaw institutional agreement between IU and a Cuban institution.

When I began as special advisor on Cuban initiatives in the IU Office of International Affairs, I couldn't have imagined that the first formal outcome would spring from a visit to my provincial birthplace, just a short distance from my former hometown of Placetas.

Nor could I have imagined that my first official role for the university would provide me the opportunity to visit Placetas for the first time since I was a child. It would be a sentimental journey, but first I had more official business in Santa Clara.

## The Queen of Radio

Before my visit to Santa Clara, Ms. Menéndez Pérez, the ICAP delegate for the province of Villa Clara, had arranged a meeting with the local chapter of the *Asociación de Pedagogos de Cuba*—Association of Cuban Educators. The meeting was scheduled to take place at the Museum of Decorative Arts of Santa Clara, which is one of several cultural institutions, including La Caridad Theater, the national José Martí library, and Hotel América, that surround Parque Vidal, the central park of Santa Clara. It is housed in a building typical of Cuban colonial architecture dating back to the eighteenth century. The building surrounds a patio and four corner gardens, which provide access to every room, including a large living room and music hall. Each room contains a collection of objects such as furniture and decorative arts characteristic of those found in wealthy Cuban homes between the eighteenth and twentieth centuries. Although we were not wealthy by any means, some of the furniture reminded me of the living room set in my grandmother's house when we lived in Placetas.

The meeting with members of the association—all of whom were educators at primary, secondary, and postsecondary levels—took place in the music hall. About twenty educators were present.

I was surprised to see that the group was especially interested in learning more about my work in alcohol and drug education and ways to prevent problems related to the abuse of alcohol and other drugs. They shared some of their own efforts and how important they considered these issues because of the need to develop better-functioning young people in the country.

The meeting was also attended by Dalia Reyes Perera, an award-winning reporter and blogger for Villa Clara's CMHW Radio, known in Cuba's central region as the Queen of Radio. Ever since second grade, Dalia had been recognized for her compositions dedicated to the people of Vietnam and the universal transcendence of Afro-American Angela Davis. In 2015, she received the Roberto González Quesada Lifetime Achievement Award on the occasion of the *Día de la*

*Prensa Cubana*—Day of the Cuban Press—in Villa Clara (González 2015). After the meeting, Dalia asked if she could interview me for her morning program, which features the island's people and events and is heard in Villa Clara and other central provinces. Some of her stories are carried nationwide by Radio Havana.

Dalia captured the essence of what had transpired at the educators' meeting. She said, "Members of the Villa Clara affiliate of the Asociación de Pedagogos de Cuba had a fruitful exchange with Gerardo González, prominent scholar of Indiana University in the city of Bloomington, United States." She noted that I was born in Placetas and emigrated with my family as a child, and she summarized my academic achievements. I had returned to my country of origin as part of a delegation of more than thirty professors and administrators from twelve American universities, which met with various Cuban institutions of higher education interested in establishing collaborative partnerships and educational agreements.

She quoted my saying that I wanted to learn more about the education system in Cuba and identify areas of common interest, that Cuba stood out for its results in student performance compared to other Latin American countries, and that I saw education as opening an important area of mutually beneficial collaboration between the two nations. She concluded her story: "Regarding the process of reestablishing relations between Cuba and the United States, he expressed that it is an opportunity to expand areas of exchange necessary for the people of both countries."

In her remarks, Dalia captured my sentiments, emphasized the positive, and promoted the point of view espoused by the Cuban government. What I did not say is that I also felt Cuban education needed to become more tolerant of dissenting points of view, something else I hope will come from more open exchanges and collaboration. I knew that back in the States, some of my Cuban compatriots and colleagues would say that I had been fooled by state propaganda. But the tolerance I advocate has to be shown on both sides of the Florida Straits. The conversations with educators in Santa Clara had only strengthened my faith and conviction that education is the key to a better and more peaceful relationship between the United States and Cuba.

In her story, Dalia also touched on the sentimental part of my trip to Villa Clara. "Gerardo indicated that he will visit his family, whom he has not seen in decades." Then she quoted my statement: "*Será un momento inolvidable, que he esperado toda la vida*—It will be an unforgettable moment, one I've waited for all my life."

# 11  But I'm from Around Here

I HAD BEEN on that road hundreds of times. When I think of my childhood in Cuba, what I remember most is the road trip on the Carretera Central between Santa Clara and Placetas—twenty-one miles of the most beautiful, lush, and scenic landscape on the island. I remember sitting in the back of the car, lost in thought or fantasy as my father drove and royal palm trees rolled by along the green hills and valleys beside the curvy road. I remember the bright-blue sky with white cloud figurines dancing high above and the frequent thunderclouds that rolled over the hills to freshen up the country smell with their summer showers. That morning, as I was leaving Santa Clara for Placetas in the old Lada with the driver and my ICAP host Miguelito, it rained, and everything, from the trees to the rocks to the road, looked and smelled clean and fresh, just as I remembered it.

Finally, I was on the road to Placetas. And just as I had been countless times as a child, I was lost in thought as Miguelito and the driver chatted in the front seat. What would it be like to enter my hometown for the first time since becoming a refugee in the Great North?

The entrance to the city where I was born is inauspicious. From Santa Clara, you have to go over a large overpass everyone in Villa Clara knows as El Elevado—the very one that held almost mythical qualities in my mind. I'd been inspired to think that if I didn't make it in this world, I could always go and live under El Elevado. It had been the subject of love letters to my wife. I reassured her that no matter what lot life would bring, we had nothing to fear because there was a place we could go.

As we approached the city limits, I could see the rising silhouette of the overpass in front of me. Before I could say anything, Miguelito turned to me and said, "Look Gerardo, there's El Elevado." And there it was—a place of a million waking dreams, right in front of me. What would I see on the other side of El Elevado? I soon found out. As we entered Placetas over El Elevado and asked for directions to my elderly aunt's home, I was horrified by the state of disrepair in the area where she lived. Her house was at the end of a dirt street, full of potholes filled with water and mud from the morning showers. It was a two-tone, blue-colored masonry house off the street, with a stream running beside it. It was surrounded by a short cinder-block fence with another wire fence atop, and metal bars blocking the entrance. The roof was made of red tile and tin. Outside the fence, on a field of overgrown weeds, lay dead branches cut from the trees that surrounded the property.

And there they were: my elderly aunt Rosa, her daughter Aida, her granddaughter Anai, and her great-grandson Eldrei, standing by the door, waiting for me. I was overwhelmed. I hugged my aunt, and we both broke down in tears. She kept feeling my face as my cousin and my aunt's granddaughter kept saying, "*Sí, es Gera; sí, es Gera*—Yes, it's Gera; yes, it's Gera." The years had taken a toll on my aunt's eyesight. She was blind.

My aunt looked well for her advanced age. Her hair was snow-white and her skin marked by years of toil, but she looked healthy. Except for the constraints imposed by blindness, she moved around well and had a very sharp mind. Her physique and demeanor reminded me a lot of my mother. Aida, Anai, and Eldrei also looked very well. They were heavyset and robust, showing no sign of poor nutrition. My cousin Aida looked to be in her sixties and was quite active, with short red hair. Anai was a young-looking, thirty-something woman with thick, curly black hair and a pleasant smile. Eldrei was sixteen years old and a sophomore in high school. He looked a lot like his mother.

I turned to Miguelito, who had walked me to the door, and introduced him to my family. Then I walked back to the car with him to thank the driver and say our goodbyes. At that moment, before Miguelito got in the car, he put his arm on my shoulder, leaned close to my ear and said, "Be careful around here." He didn't say it, but I'm sure the dire conditions of the neighborhood where he dropped me off had made an impression on him. This was no tourist town. He told me not to wander off, because if anything were to happen to me, ICAP would be responsible. He also asked me to please call him if anything happened.

Be careful? What would I need to be careful about? I was home. And why would ICAP be responsible for me? I was with my family. Although somewhat shocked by the sudden warning, I didn't give it much thought. I said I'd be fine, waved goodbye, and returned to the door where my family was still standing. Inside the house, they showed me around and told me they had divided the small house into two quarters: one for my aunt Anai and her husband, who was at work, and one for Aida and Eldrei. Aida and Eldrei shared a small bedroom past a small living room at the entrance to the house. Everyone shared a small kitchen and two small bathrooms. There was no hot water in the house.

Aida said she would move over to Anai's side of the house during my stay and I could sleep in her bed next to Eldrei. She asked me to put my bags down anywhere in the room and join them on the small patio outside the kitchen that the family shared as a dining room, where lunch would be served.

Before lunch, I wanted to buy a cake for my aunt. That day, she was celebrating her ninety-third birthday. I quickly learned that buying a cake in Placetas is not like going to a local bakery in the United States. I was told there was a small place that sold crackers and other foodstuffs a few blocks from the corner that might have cake, but they weren't sure. Eager to take a walk around the neighborhood,

I said I'd check it out and asked for directions. My cousin said Eldrei would go with me as he was known in the town and could help avoid problems. Problems? What problems? I said I'd go on my own, but Aida and Anai insisted Eldrei go with me. As we started our trek to the store, Eldrei told me there had been a couple of knifings recently, and the town had become quite dangerous for outsiders. I didn't say anything; I just thought to myself, But I'm from around here.

Eldrei and I went to a couple of places in search of a cake, but none were to be found. Instead, I purchased some sweets and candies. When we returned, Anai had prepared a lovely traditional meal, including black bean soup, which awaited us at the table on the patio. I was surprised at what happened next. As soon as the aroma of her lovely food began to fill the house and the yard, neighbors started gathering with cups. She told them what soup she was cooking, and they held out their cups while she filled them from the large cooking pot. This scene repeated itself every day as neighbors came by at lunchtime, cup in hand, inquiring which soup Anai had made that day. They gave her a little money and went away happy.

After lunch, Aida and I devised a plan to visit my special childhood places and all my cousins who lived in Placetas. I was filled with anticipation.

## First Night in Placetas

On my first night in Placetas, something happened that concerned me, and which has been on my mind ever since. When I went to bed, I felt anxious, uncertain, and insecure. I could not fall asleep. I'd gone to Placetas excited and elated, overjoyed at the thought of seeing my old hometown once again. Memories had flooded back of the happiness I'd felt as a child, the safety and exhilaration of living in a warm and friendly town … a safe and secure place.

I had pushed from my mind Miguelito's warning to be careful, and Eldrei's admonition that it was a dangerous place for strangers. Suddenly, in the quiet of the night, as I lay in bed, their words came thundering back. I began to wonder why all those fences around the house were necessary, and whether the steel bars at the door would be enough to keep out an intruder. In Cuba, Americans can't use credit cards, so I carried quite a lot of cash. Now I was worried that somebody would enter the bedroom, knowing that a wealthy stranger was staying there. Yet this was my hometown, my city, the place where I'd felt safe and protected as a child. What was happening? Was I really an outsider?

Eventually, I fell asleep. The next morning, I happily woke to a rooster's crow outside my window. I was excited to be going out to see people and places that had been little more than faint memories and yet so much a part of me. But last night's fear stayed with me. I had become much more sensitive to the way locals looked at me. I realized that they did indeed know I was not from around here. I was glad to be accompanied by my cousin Aida, who was well known in Placetas. Everyone we encountered on the streets was friendly but

Street view in Placetas from the back of a horse-drawn taxi.

aloof toward me, or simply stayed away. I felt strange as I had years ago, when kids in Miami and Pittsburgh pointed their fingers at me because I was an outsider, a refugee.

## Visiting the Cousins

Aida and I walked everywhere we went, except when we took one of the horse-drawn carriages that serve as taxis and are the main mode of public transportation in Placetas. The carriages were a great way to see the city and feel its ambiance. The typical carriage seats two passengers. A driver in front steers the horse. As we rode through the streets to our various destinations, Aida called attention to various points of interest. Sometimes I just looked around as people went about their everyday lives. When we were not talking, the only thing I heard was the constant "tac-tac, tac-tac, tac-tac" of horseshoes hitting the road and the rhythmic voice of the driver calling out *"caballo, caballo*—horse, horse" to keep the beast under control. Everything seemed surreal, as if an old movie were unfolding before my eyes.

Either walking or traveling by carriage, Aida and I made our way to visit all my cousins in Placetas. I had eight cousins, including Aida and her brother Pepe.

Four of my cousins lived with their extended families, two lived by themselves, and two lived with each other. In Miami, my mother had given me some money for three of my cousins who were especially hard-pressed financially. I also gave some personal cash to everyone we visited—except for two cousins who were doing well—because it was clear they needed and welcomed the gift. One of our first visits was to my cousin Chechi, one of three men in the group, who was hosting his two daughters and two grandchildren who were visiting from Havana. One daughter was a medical doctor and the other, a physical therapist. Yet from the look of his surroundings, he seemed impoverished, and his house seemed to be in dire need of repair. Although his daughters were professionals, they didn't earn much money and could not help him out. He was grateful for the little cash I gave him.

In fact, I was surprised how readily all of my cousins accepted the money, though perhaps I shouldn't have been. Gifts of money—remittances—from relatives in the United States have become part of Cubans' way of life, and one of the country's primary sources of hard currency. Such gifts are not seen as charity. Instead, they're what those privileged to live in the Great North do for impoverished families on the island. It was obvious that my cousins who were doing relatively well had close relatives in the United States. Still, their crowded living conditions and way of life made it clear that theirs was a hard existence.

## A Childhood Friend

In between family visits, Aida took me to places that held special meaning. I was particularly excited to go to a place where I remember growing up: my grandparents' home. Perhaps because it was inherited through my grandmother's side of the family, we always called it *abuela's*—grandmother's—or Yeya's house, after the nickname I'd given my grandmother. Yet what I remembered didn't exist. In those distant days, it was a white wooden structure, set back from the street. But the new owners had significantly remodeled it, and it looked the same as the other adjoining houses. Next door was the house of my best friend in Cuba, Hugo Morales. Hugo and I had grown up together, and our families were very close, but over the years I had lost touch with him. I was surprised to learn that Hugo still lived next door to my grandmother's house. I knocked on his door and a young man holding a baby greeted me. I asked for Hugo, and to my surprise, he said he was Hugo. Then he said, "Oh, you must mean my father."

I told young Hugo who I was and, before I could say another word, he said, "Oh yes, my father often talks about you. I'll get him." When my old friend came into the front room, we didn't need introductions. We saw each other, and with tears in our eyes, embraced for what seemed like an eternity.

Hugo and I spoke for a while, then he looked into my eyes and said, "I have a confession to make." He asked if I remembered that we used to play cards. When I said I did, he said, "Well, I once cheated on you." He went on to explain that he had set the deck so that I would draw a high hand at poker and bet heavily, while he held a higher hand. We laughed at this confession, but I wondered how long he'd carried the guilt of cheating on his closest friend, not knowing whether he'd ever have the chance to set the record straight. It was a very small thing for two young children at play, but I could tell his confession had taken a load off his chest. I was happy for that.

Then Hugo invited me to go into the yard that his and my grandmother's houses shared at the back, where we had spent many hours as children, climbing trees and playing games. As we walked into the yard, he pointed to an empty spot and said, "Remember the mango tree that was there?" Before I could respond, he said, "It was blown down by the last hurricane." Then he pointed to another spot. He said, "That's where your father used to fix cars before he opened his auto repair shop. Look here. I have a surprise for you."

We looked over the property line into my grandmother's yard, and there, lying behind some rubbish, he pointed out a big, barrel-like block of wood about two feet high. It was the hub of a wheel from the huge *carretas*—wagons that transported sugarcane from the fields to the sugar mills in Cuba.

I was mystified until Hugo explained that my father had used this very hub more than fifty years ago in his car repair business. "When your dad hoisted cars up on jacks to work underneath them and repair them, he never trusted the jacks. Instead, he used to put this hub under the cars in case the jacks failed and the car fell down. Then he knew he wouldn't be crushed."

What he said was so matter-of-fact, yet it was a life-and-death moment for my father, and it brought back to me two things. The first was that my father had been such a dedicated, hard worker all his life, who made do with whatever tools he had. I was touched that I could return to Florida and tell him what I'd seen. The second was that nothing in Cuba had changed since he'd left. He could almost have stepped back after half a century and picked up where he'd left off.

That was vividly brought home when Hugo took me next door to meet the current residents of my grandmother's old house. Amazingly, the electricity bills were still in my grandfather's name, and even the furniture in the living room had belonged to my grandmother.

It was getting late, and I told Hugo we had to move on. He wanted me to come back the next day to have dinner with his family, but I said it wasn't possible because of my short stay. I told him I had an old picture of our families that I had scanned and would drop off a copy before I left. He said he would be there.

As promised, the next morning I stopped by. The photo showed our families together with a young Hugo and me. When I handed it to him, it was as if an angel had descended from heaven and lifted his spirits. As he gazed in amazement at the photo, he had to sit down, and a radiant smile lit up his face. I don't know if or when I'll see Hugo again, but our childhood friendship had been rekindled. I'll never forget that day and the look on Hugo's face as I walked away.

## A Stop in the Old Neighborhood

The previous night, when we left Hugo's house on the way to my aunt's, Aida and I had walked around the corner to the house my family had lived in before emigrating. It was late and getting dark, but it was only a short walk, and I couldn't wait to see it. Like most other streets in Placetas, my old street was in total disrepair; it looked like a war zone. A corner bodega where as a child I used to buy candy and other snacks had been blown down by a hurricane and never rebuilt. A creek that flowed through the corner was polluted and overgrown with weeds, and walls that used to keep the waters from overflowing during heavy rains had fallen into the creek. The houses were covered with mildew, and many were crumbling. Small gardens in front of the houses had reverted to patches of dirt or been overtaken by invasive weeds. A small drainage ditch that ran in front of the houses along the street to the corner creek was stagnant and filled with dirt. The mud holes on the street were almost impassable; Aida and I had to jump over the potholes just to make our way.

That's not how I remember my old street. Placetas has some of the widest streets in Cuba. On that street I remember playing pick-up baseball games with other kids. There was no way we could play a pick-up game in that street today. Ironically, the only house that was under reconstruction was the one I used to live in. It was a little white duplex with a small front porch filled with sandbags and debris from the demolition underway inside. We approached the house. The owner, his wife, and their son were standing outside, and I introduced myself. I said I'd lived in the house they now occupied, but had left for the United States more than fifty years ago, and was back in Placetas for the first time. The owner said I wouldn't know anyone in the neighborhood—those who'd lived there the longest had been there only forty years.

I reminisced a bit and said I was sorry to see that the small drainage ditch in front of the house had been filled. I told him, "When it rained, I used to place little paper boats on the ditch and run after them until I saw them disappear on the large corner creek." He replied, "Well, now, when it rains, the whole street floods."

I was heartbroken by the condition of the old neighborhood I remembered so fondly. If I hadn't known where I was standing, I wouldn't have recognized it. As we walked away, I looked back down the street one more time, and thanked God for the memories.

## Getting Around Town

After dropping off Hugo's photo, Aida and I set out to see other sights that held special meaning for me. First, we went to El Elevado. As we approached the El Elevado overpass at street level on one of the unpaved roads that run below it, we saw people going about their business and an occasional car or truck traveling on the road above. My heart beat faster and faster with excitement as we got closer to El Elevado; I wanted to see whether destitute people still lived under it, as I remembered. Or were those visions just a product of my imagination? Sometimes we imagine things we believe to be true. But those images were so real to me. Could they have been part of a dream? I was getting nervous because from a distance, I saw no signs of life.

I had to know whether the picture I'd held onto most of my life of a place I could always go if things didn't work out—a place that had inspired me to work hard, but not fear failure—had any basis in reality. Lo and behold, it did.

Imagine my sense of relief when, tucked under a corner of the overpass, I spotted a makeshift shelter of scrapped wooden boards carefully placed one atop the other, to provide protection from the elements. The overpass served as a roof, and the dirt below, a floor. A perfectly square window had been crafted and secured with metal bars, like the ones I saw around windows in houses all over town. The doors were also made out of carefully placed boards that ran perpendicular to the walls. One led to what looked like a storage area. Sitting on the corner on a makeshift stool was a man who appeared to be the resident. He looked to be in his mid-sixties or early seventies and wore black penny loafers, white socks, black pants, a Cuban-style guayabera white shirt open at the top, and a black cap. He had thick eyebrows and a thick mustache that partially covered the subtle smile on his face.

Not far from him was an old bicycle that seemed to be in good condition, which surely provided him the transportation he needed. Strung on the bicycle handlebars was a blue handbag for carrying small items of food or other possessions.

This man looked happy and content, so much so that I didn't want to disturb him with questions about what it was like to live under El Elevado. I had seen it with my own eyes—proof positive that it was possible to live under El Elevado and be happy.

Aida and I smiled at the man and continued along the side of the bypass toward the center of town. Our next destination: El Parque de Los Laureles—a place that also held many memories. Gone were the hundreds of metal chairs and benches I remembered so well, replaced around the park with a sparse selection of iron and wooden benches colored in blue and green. In one corner of the park stood *El Rincón de las Madres*—The Mother's Corner, with its two serpentine stone benches and the statue of the Virgin Mary, holding a child in her arms. The big laurel trees, for which the park is known, lined the park's perimeter. They seemed less majestic and lush, but still added to the park's beauty. The old band shell at the center of the park, where I had attended many concerts as a child, had been replaced with a modernistic structure that seemed out of place. Still surrounding the band shell stood the eight royal palms planted in memory of eight students executed by the Spanish during the War of Independence.

I did see signs of change in the vicinity of the park. The most visible, directly across the street from El Rincón de las Madres, was a newly renovated San Atanasio de Placetas Catholic Church, named after the town's patron saint and the only freshly painted building in sight. Just down the road a buzzing *Area de Comercialización Trabajadores por Cuenta Propia*—Area of Commercialization for Private Enterprise Workers—was packed with customers buying all sorts of things—fake jewelry, hats, produce, plumbing supplies, and more. The only empty store I saw was the state-run *Mini Mercado Centro*—Central Mini Mart. Walking in the commercialization area, I noticed an old boarded-up hotel and took a photo from across the street. Someone leaned over me from behind and whispered, "*Tirale, tirale, fotos para que todos vean la porquería que han hecho de esto*—Go ahead, go ahead and take photos so everyone can see the crap they've made out of this place."

I chuckled at the stranger's sense of humor.

## The Most Personal Encounter

Nothing brought home the irony of how my family's fortunes had changed since I was a kid, exiled from everything I knew and loved, more than my father's taller in Placetas.

At first, I didn't recognize the place. It had been turned into a *Punto de Venta No. 3, El Mango*—Point of Sale No. 3, El Mango—a state-run fruit and vegetable stand. A sign with big white letters on a red background in front of the counter welcomed buyers with the slogan: "*Siempre es el 26*—It is always the 26th," referring to the revolution's 26th of July movement. I had to walk around for a while to make sure I was really standing in my father's old auto repair shop. An inside wall had been built across the facility. The front served as a display and point-of-sale area for the produce, and the back was a warehouse. Only when I passed through the door in the wall into the warehouse section did I recognize the facility as my father's taller.

I had been to that shop hundreds, if not thousands, of times. I could still smell in my mind the burning torches, brake fluid, acid, gasoline, grease, and other pungent substances, the staples of my father's work in that space, that had marked his hands as those of a mechanic.

My emotions were profoundly mixed as I saw the place he'd been so proud of. I hadn't been back in half a century. Seeing how much it had changed, I was hit by feelings of surprise, bemusement, shock, and sadness. There, on the wall of my father's shop over the caption "*Volverán*—They shall return," was a painting of the Cuban Five, who'd been feted by Cuba as heroes of the revolution but imprisoned in the United States, accused of espionage and conspiracy to commit murder. As if that wasn't ironic enough, alongside a picture of Che Guevara was a quote from José Martí, extolling the virtues of hard work: "*El trabajo no es más que acuñar las ideas en oro y plata*—Work is only to stamp ideas in gold and silver."

The irony was numbing. Nobody in Placetas had worked harder than my father. He left early to go to work each day and rarely came home before dark. He did all the heavy work himself, without staff or modern machinery. Yet we left Cuba viewed as gusanos by those in power under the revolutionary government. And now, almost fifty-four years later, I was reading signs on the walls of my father's shop that said only through hard work could the revolution succeed.

Did the people who put up those slogans have any idea how hard my father had toiled inside these walls so his family could survive?

Did those in charge have any idea that they'd turned one of the most beautiful places on earth into one whose streets turned to rivers when it rained, whose buildings were crumbling, and whose citizens have to "resolver" every day in order to get by?

Many in Cuba blame the US embargo—the "*bloqueo*," as they call it—for the economic failures of the system. It certainly hasn't helped improve conditions on the island. But the truth is more complicated. In the years since I returned to Cuba in 2012, although many still fear the system and pessimism about change abounds, I've seen some cautious optimism grow among the people. The thaw in US–Cuba relations promises a new chapter in the history of two countries that are culturally, geographically, and politically intertwined. Although the election of Donald Trump as president of the United States in 2016 and his subsequent announcement of changes to US policy toward Cuba slowed down the process of normalization between the two countries, they did not completely stop the progress made under the Obama administration. Nevertheless, moving forward with better relations will require sensitivity, understanding, forgiveness, and, yes, a lot of hard work.

My nostalgia at returning to my roots was dulled by seeing the conditions in which some of my family lived, the overall state of disrepair in the town, and my fear at realizing that others considered me an outsider. But I'm from around here, I kept telling myself.

In reality, I was in my hometown as a Cuban American. As much as I consider myself a Villareño and Placeteño, I cannot separate my experience from that of a US citizen. I owe much to the United States for the opportunities it has afforded my family and me. Yet I am also proud of my Cuban heritage.

I have now traveled more miles and seen more places in Cuba as a Cuban American than in my eleven years as a child on the island. I've also traveled the world and have brought back to Cuba a different perspective because of the education I received in the United States. I've seen firsthand the transformative power of education. Without it, I couldn't have realized my parents' dreams for me, for which they sacrificed so much.

I hope that through education I can in some meaningful way help foster a process of reconciliation between my native country and my adopted homeland. No, I don't agree with or support everything that goes on in Cuba under Communism, just as I don't agree with or support everything that goes on in the United States.

Visiting Placetas underscored how right my parents were to decide to leave when they did. We were unjustly accused of being gusanos, and my father lost the ability to do what he loved most: productive work.

But that was Cuba's reality in the days of the revolution. Perhaps in the future, things will be different. Perhaps …

## Parental Sentiments

Yes, it was thrilling for me to visit my former hometown and along the way foster a new IU partnership with a leading university in Villa Clara. But I also felt a deep sadness, unsure how my parents would feel about the welcome I received as a leader, trying to better US-Cuba relations. I wondered whether they would feel betrayed, or hurt, or proud. They had forsaken their land and its socialist system so my sister and I could have a better life.

I couldn't wait to get back to Miami to tell my parents about my visit and ask them about their feelings. I was elated when they both said they were happy to know things had gone well and I was learning about my birthplace. But like the dancer at the Opera de la Calle in Havana, they, too, didn't trust the US–Cuba thaw, and doubted that my efforts at educational partnerships would bring systemic change any time soon. Nevertheless, my father said, "*Ojalá que tengas suerte con eso*—I wish you luck with that."

Before my initial trip to Cuba in 2012, I asked my parents whether they regretted immigrating to the United States. Without hesitation, my father said, "No, no, no. This really turned out to be the greatest country on earth. At first it was difficult. But with each passing year, we've developed and grown, especially you and Mari. Back there I remember you as a *gallito*—a small fighting cock—but here you've become a man. I would do it all over again."

During that earlier conversation, we spoke about our lives in Cuba and I commented on how monumental it had been to receive the telegram that granted us permission to leave the country. My father just shrugged and said that after a yearlong effort to get a visa waiver from the US Department of State, the telegram "*fue lo último*—was the last thing." He went to the back of the house and returned with an old briefcase. To my surprise, he pulled out the very document. "I still have the telegram here."

I was amazed. My father had kept that telegram for more than fifty years. Now, after visiting Santa Clara and Placetas, I wanted to know more: Had his feelings about leaving Cuba changed since our conversation in 2012? Did he regret never going back to Cuba? Would he like to visit Placetas again? To all three questions, he said affirmatively, "No."

Then he went back into the old briefcase and pulled from it the silver peso he had carried with him when we left Cuba. It was a 1934 Cuban coin embossed with the famous slogan: "*Patria y Libertad*—Fatherland and Liberty." He said, "I've kept it all these years for good luck. *Ahora es tuyo*—Now it's yours."

# 12  To You, the Immigrant

Writing this memoir caused me to reflect deeply on my experiences as an immigrant and on the factors that helped me achieve the American Dream. It made me more sensitive to the plight of migrants and refugees everywhere, especially during these turbulent times. Today, millions upon millions of people throughout the world are leaving their homelands, seeking refuge from violence, political persecution, starvation, economic deprivation, and hopelessness. Many look toward the United States as an historically welcoming nation and a land of opportunity.

America is a country of immigrants—generation after generation of immigrants—all of whom entered the United States with many of the same feelings of uncertainty, fear, and anxiety that migrants and refugees everywhere experience. Yet, they built this country into one of the greatest nations on earth. Through opportunity and appropriate support, the vast majority of immigrants have become contributing citizens and role models for future generations.

Adolfo Carrión Jr., a businessman and former elected official from City Island, New York City, says this about his family's immigration experience:

"This may sound cliché to some, but for my family it's not. In one generation we went from parents with little formal education to all four kids graduating from graduate school and going on to successful professions. I have no doubt that my kids will achieve and contribute even more to the American enterprise. This is what keeps me going: that you can go from a sub-basement apartment in a 1960s Brooklyn ghetto to working for the president of the United States in one generation." (United States Citizenship 2016)

There are countless stories of immigrants who came with nothing and turned their lives around. Jerry Yang, the founder of Yahoo, was born in Taipei, Taiwan, in 1968, and immigrated to the United States with his family at the age of eight. He knew only one word of English: "shoe." Andrew Ly, the founder of Sugar Bowl Bakery, fled Vietnam and, after nine months in a Malaysian refugee camp, arrived in the United States in 1979. For eight years, he lived in a two-bedroom apartment with his extended family while he learned English (Goldschein 2012).

When I examine my own trajectory from bullied, isolated kid to leading American educator, I find several key influences that contributed to my success. Chief among these: a loving and supportive family, a community that provided me a sense of belonging, and caring mentors who guided me along the way. I believed in taking advantage of what life brings rather than being bound by fixed goals, being willing to take a leap of faith when unsure where to turn, finding and pursuing a passion with vigor, listening to others who care, remembering my roots, and giving back. These attitudes led to opportunities that enriched my life. I conclude this memoir with some reflections on these influences and beliefs. I hope my experiences—and perhaps a bit of unsolicited advice—can provide helpful guidance and support to new immigrants, refugees, and other life voyagers struggling to fit in.

## Never Give Up

A major part of my motivation and support system was my family. Through the worst times, we knew we loved each other, bore each other up. We drew strength from each other. When my parents briefly considered sending my sister Maritza to the United States alone, with the rest of us to follow, my mother quickly rejected that idea. Our strength came from staying together as family. Our support for each other got us through the extended times without work, the coldest times in Pittsburgh, and the bullying in school. No matter how tough times were, I had the companionship of my sister and parents who made us feel loved, who reassured us that somehow everything would be all right.

There were times I wanted to give up, drop out of school and society. In small ways, I did, when I sat mute in the classroom in Miami after being publicly humiliated by the vice principal's *buena conducta*. What kept me from giving up altogether were my family's examples of hope and resilience. The countless times my family moved in search of work and a better life: leaving our home in Cuba, then going from Miami, to Pittsburgh, to New Jersey, and back to Miami. Those were acts of courage and of hope, examples of the value of continually trying for something better. My parents never let the dark times define them. I couldn't let them down by giving up. So, I asked myself: Why shouldn't I keep trying, too? As a child, I remember my mother constantly telling us that no matter how bad our lot, something good would come of it. *"Gera, acuerdate, no hay mal que por bien no venga*—Gera, remember, there is no harm from which some good won't come."* In other words, "Every cloud has a silver lining."

When my early school experiences turned me into a kid who sat mute in the back of the class in Miami, then simply tolerated high school, waiting till I could finally put school behind me, the school system forgot about me. I became invisible, tracked into a vocational program I had no interest in. But I had to keep going. Many times, my father spoke of education as the way to a better life for poor people. His voice rang in my ears, telling me that with an education, we could improve ourselves, look forward to a brighter future. But the lesson he instilled in me went deeper than language. It was the image of his working man's hands. His hands were a vivid symbol. When I got discouraged, I'd remember his words, his hands, the sacrifices he and my mother and my grandparents made, all so we could have a better life.

With my parents' support and encouragement, I pursued an education, and it transformed my life. In a democratic society, education truly is the great equalizer. Pursue an education. Never give up.

Find Community

As our immigrant family moved from city to city, I felt like an outsider. I didn't belong. I longed for local communities of other immigrants, or people who spoke my language, to serve as safe and trusted groups with whom I could discuss common problems and ideas for making my way. In West New York, New Jersey, I discovered other Spanish-speaking kids. Suddenly I had a peer group, people who understood my language and my culture. That young community brought me out of my shell. I began to develop confidence and inner strength. At the University of Florida, I overheard some students speaking Spanish, I introduced myself, and we bonded instantly. In those communities I found others who had experience with the kinds of challenges I faced, and gave practical advice about resources such as housing, schools, and libraries. As members of a community, sharing stories, experiences, and ideas, we formed a kind of extended family of trusted listeners who empathized with each other and had each other's interests at heart. And when we needed to be heard, to advocate for shared interests, the voice of many carried more power than the voice of one.

Being part of a community can help immigrants and others who are different withstand prejudice and the damage it can cause. I think back to an experience early in my academic career, during a visit to La Paz, Bolivia. A young girl in our discussion group wept over the fact that her indigenous facial features would forever mark her as inadequate and stunt her chances in life. The bullying I experienced as a child was based in prejudice. I was different: I looked and sounded different. When I was able to band together with kids like myself in West New York, New Jersey, I felt good about myself for the first time in my life. Once mute, now I talked all the time. I gained in confidence. On top of being "different," we were also adolescents, struggling with painful rites of passage. In our little group of Spanish-speakers, we supported each other through our identity crises and the prejudice we encountered.

At the University of Florida in Gainesville, I stuck out amid the predominantly white student population. Not only did the campus lack diversity, but there were no special services for Hispanic students. Our small group of Cuban students was our own tight-knit social and support group. And in the long term, when it came time to advocate for a new Institute for Hispanic and Latino Cultures and special services for Latino students, we were successful because we were able to speak with one voice.

Find a community that makes you feel you belong. Reach out and get involved.

## Seek Mentors

Having a mentor or mentors can make an enormous difference in a person's life. My first true mentor was Marvin Levine at The Rouge boutique in Miami, where I held a part-time job during high school. I treated that job like it was the most important job I'd ever do, and it paid off. Mr. Levine recognized my work ethic and my flair for retail, and he encouraged me. He took me under his wing and taught me how to manage the store, buy clothes, and help people find what looked good on them. Under his guidance, I discovered something I loved, developed a talent for it, and built a dream for a future in fashion. It's unimportant that my dream didn't pan out. What mattered was the confidence I gained by learning a new skill. I formed a relationship with Mr. Levine and earned the trust of an expert who passed his knowledge on to me. My relationship with Mr. Levine was the first of many important relationships with individuals who became mentors.

As my professors Dr. Van Hartesveldt and Dr. Swanson did at the University of Florida, mentors helped me discover talents I didn't know I had, opened doors for me, provided guidance and encouragement, gave me confidence, and even became trusted friends. Dr. Thomas Goodale guided me into a profession. He saw the difference I could make. He trusted and empowered me to be a leader, to organize students and rally them to work for effective solutions to an intractable problem that causes untold misery to individuals and society. His mentoring led to a movement that changed the equation on how we deal with alcohol abuse on campus and inspires young people to play a positive role.

Seek and take advantage of mentors. They can change your life. To paraphrase Henry Adams's famous quote about the influence of teachers, "A mentor affects eternity; he can never tell where his influence stops."

## Trust Serendipity

Our society today puts a premium on setting goals for ourselves and our future. Many feel that setting goals gives shape and direction to their future. Some people know from a young age exactly what they want to do; others, like me, find it difficult to formulate long-term plans to serve as guides. Setting goals isn't for everyone. I didn't set goals; instead I always trusted fate, or karma—whatever you may call it. My path of work unfolded almost organically. From each experience I learned something that enabled me to take a next appropriate step. The fashion boutique was a random circumstance—a part-time job that fell into my lap. From that job, I learned that I could learn, that I could excel and, like my father, could feel passionate about a career.

College was the next surprising development. Going to college had never occurred to me. I wasn't "college material." But then came my friend Rafael's chance remark: Gerardo, why don't you go to college? This was fate again, sending me a message. Working in the group home led me to graduate school. The graduate assistantship where I had the opportunity to work with leaders in my field augmented my interest in doing my own research. What characterizes all these examples is that in every case, I threw myself wholeheartedly into my work. If I failed at something, I was motivated to try harder. I believe that if you put your heart and soul into whatever passion you pursue, one thing can lead to another, and as you discover more about your talents and interests, your path can grow organically.

When I faced going to college, I wondered: What if I fail? It can be easy to slip into worrying and believing you can't do something. I tried not to think too far ahead; instead, I just took the next right step and watched where it took me. Those new experiences provided me with information, clues, answers, and even opportunities to learn and discover something about myself. I trusted that by taking one step after another, and staying present in the moment and alert to opportunities, I would find a path I could trust.

Sometimes serendipity steps in and provides an opportunity. I think of my grandfather, a templero, who was out of work. He happened to stop in at a café frequented by sugarcane workers. One of the bosses had a technical problem, and my grandfather happened to have an idea that provided a solution. My grandfather was offered a job the next day. That chance encounter turned his life around. Any conversation, random meeting, or relationship has the potential to open doors to opportunity if you stay alert to possibility.

## Ask Questions

Rafael's suggestion to go to college came out of left field. I was afraid to try. But I was more afraid not to try. I had no clue how to approach getting into college. My parents had inspired and encouraged me to get an education, but I knew they couldn't help me with the admissions process. Rafael's wisdom and experience were my aid.

Going to the Miami Dade Junior College Admissions Office took me far beyond my comfort zone. When I walked through that door, I wondered if they would recognize my lack of preparation. Would I know what questions to ask? Entering the building took courage. But walking in was the hardest part. Again, when it came time to choose a major, I found myself at sea. I had questions about not only my major, but also about my identity, and my likes and dislikes. I found help from another group of advisors at the Counseling and Career Services Center, which offered tests that could help me define my interests. But I didn't know how to take the tests. Was I ever embarrassed about that! Yet, here was a chance to learn something about myself, so rather than simply guess, I asked the counselor how to go about answering the questions.

Taking small steps like these helped me find tools, people, and resources that guided me in my quest for education. I discovered that people in helping professions, like college counselors, advisors, and clergy, genuinely want to help, not judge. I found that if I had the courage to ask questions, people would help me. The greatest challenge was overcoming the fear of taking the first step, that leap of faith.

Taking similar small steps can help you, too. Don't be afraid to ask questions, no matter how naïve they may seem. Asking the right questions can turn your life around.

## Pursue Your Passion

My father was a brilliant mechanic. His ability to restore old cars to pristine showroom condition was a gift. The way he used his skills and the pride he took in his work were an inspiration to me. I saw the rewards of doing something you love. Working at The Rouge, I experienced those feelings for the first time. What pride I took in my work. Working at the boys' group home was an opportunity to turn my painful childhood experiences into empathy, support, and nurture for boys who, to an extent, reminded me of myself as a kid. Here was an opportunity to create value from something I'd rather have forgotten. And because I empathized, I was good at this work. Helping people became a passion, and it led me to graduate school. When you find something you love, find a way to pursue it.

## Listen to Others

I was fortunate to have a strong family—multiple generations of people who saw hard work as a source of pride, who never gave up trying to find work that they could excel at and be proud of. I drew strength from my family's steadfast belief that they had something of value to offer. Not everyone's background includes that kind of model. But everyone can find in their past a teacher, a friend, or a boss who complimented them on a job well done and who recognized that they were good at something. Someone who said: I wish I could do that as well as you do. We are told these things, but often they don't sink in, or we simply take our skills for granted. Listen to those special people who recognize your talents, and take their encouragement to heart.

## Remember Your Roots

When I became an academic leader and dean of education at one of America's premier universities, I did not forget my humble beginnings. Throughout my tenure, many faculty, staff, alumni, and students commented on my accessibility and, as one senior administrator put it, "your soft touch." I'm not sure what that meant, but I always treated everyone with dignity and respect. I believe in the worth of every individual and I never let whatever power and influence I had get in the way of treating everyone kindly, equitably, and fairly.

Treating everyone with dignity is something my parents taught and encouraged me to do. The roots of those lessons were especially brought home to me by the story my father told about my grandfather taking him to his cousins' home to see if they had a pair of shoes they could spare. The pain I saw in my father's eyes as he told the story and his emphasis on the fact that "we had gone to ask but not to beg" reminded me that whatever one's lot in life, being proud of oneself is important (and fragile). I wanted to make sure everyone I worked with—from the groundskeeper to the tech staff to the superstar professor—felt proud of the contributions they made to the organization.

It is easy to bring someone down; it is much harder to build someone up. Doing everything possible to recognize others is a hallmark of effective leadership. Remember to offer a kind word, a simple "good morning," or a smile to those whose paths you cross. It could brighten their day, and yours.

## Give Back

As an immigrant and a refugee, I experienced separation from extended family and friends, isolation, prejudice, and many of the fears and anxieties common to those who are forced to leave their homeland. But with the support of my parents, friends, mentors, and communities that embraced me, I was able to get an education, achieve a position of influence and leadership, meet the challenges of being different, and give back to others. I'm proud of the letter I received from the president of the United States commending me for the "fine contribution" I made to young people in my adopted homeland.

When I was given the opportunity to go back to my native Cuba as an ambassador for my university, I did not hesitate. I didn't go back with rancor for the painful memories or hatred in my heart. Instead, I wanted to make a positive difference—to help heal the wounds of the past and make things better for those who remained on the island and those who welcomed me with open arms across the Florida Straits. If my efforts help foster reconciliation and bring the people of both nations closer together through education, then, from my perspective, it's all worth it.

My family, including my children and their children, have benefited greatly from the freedom and opportunities afforded us. Nothing would bring me greater joy than doing the same thing for others in need.

If you achieve great things, you, too, will find that "it is better to give than to receive." Do your part; ask yourself: what difference can I make? Give back in whatever way you can.

Do Good

As I was completing this memoir, I received the news that Fidel Castro, the commander in chief of Cuba's revolution, had died. There were spontaneous celebrations among members of the Cuban American community in Miami. In Cuba, the news was met with mourning by some and indifference by others. I asked my father how he felt about Castro's death, and he said, "I used to wish he were dead. But as time passed, I began to wish him a long life." He continued, "He'd had to live with his conscience."

So will we all. Seek to do good.

# Epilogue

Writing this memoir brought me closer to my family. It led to conversations with my parents about people and events I had heard about throughout my life, but never discussed with them in detail. These conversations helped me appreciate the great sacrifices my parents made and how those sacrifices laid the foundations that shaped me into the man I am today. I believe they also shed light on the universal aspirations of parents everywhere for freedom and a better life for their children.

My immigrant family was fortunate. America welcomed us with open arms. I was given the gift of a great education; I achieved something, and I can now give back to my adopted homeland and the world. My story shows that in the United States, as in other democratic countries, education is still the great equalizer. It is the solution to the greatest and most intractable problems facing the world today, tomorrow, and in the foreseeable future. As Nelson Mandela famously said, "Education is the most powerful weapon we can use to change the world."

Today powerful forces want us to forget that our country was founded by immigrants, our citizenry unimaginably enriched over the centuries by those who sought opportunity and a better life in this great nation. Many we consider notable Americans arrived here as immigrants. When education ignited their minds and imaginations, they bloomed into the luminaries we are proud to call our own. John James Audubon, American ornithologist, artist, and naturalist, famous for his studies of North American birds, was born in what is now Haiti. Nobel Prize-winner Albert Einstein, likely the most influential physicist of the twentieth century, was born in Germany in 1879. Henry Kissinger's family fled Germany in 1938 to escape Nazi terrorism. After receiving a PhD at Harvard, Kissinger served as national security adviser and secretary of state for Richard Nixon and Gerald Ford and received the Nobel Peace Prize for the Paris Peace Accord. Hilda Solis, the twenty-fifth US secretary of labor, was raised by parents who immigrated from Nicaragua and Mexico. She was the first female recipient of the John F. Kennedy Profile in Courage Award and the first Hispanic woman to serve in the US presidential cabinet.

As we look to the future, we should remain conscious of our historical openness and count on the contributions of those who choose to exercise their talents here. Far too many nations throughout the world are closing doors, raising the sign: "Refugees and Immigrants Not Welcome Here." What if host nations granted these immigrants the opportunity to reap the benefits I and so many others enjoyed? What if they were given that first leg up toward the privileges of citizenship and education? What educators, scientists, artists, mothers, fathers, coaches, scout leaders, school bus drivers, chefs, mental health workers, counselors, entrepreneurs, farmers, and technologists are we missing out on because we fear difference and multiculturalism?

America should not close its doors to immigrants and refugees. Now, more than ever, is the time to take stock of what our great-grandparents understood so well—that refugees and immigrants aren't drains on the capital of American society; rather, if given opportunity, they can be the future of society. Our future as a nation in an increasingly complex and diverse world still depends on being the land of opportunity—a nation still committed to the words prominently displayed on the pedestal of the Statue of Liberty, "Give me your tired, your poor, your huddled masses yearning to breathe free."

# Bibliography

Bartlett, Kay. 1977. "Little Havana On the Hudson." *Pittsburgh Post-Gazette*, June 28. Accessed September 20, 2016. https://news.google.com/newspapers?nid=1129&dat=1977 0628&id=4kwNAAAAIBAJ&sjid=U2oDAAAAIBAJ&pg=4464,3136176&hl=en.

Birman, Dina and Meredith Poff. 2011. "Intergenerational Differences in Acculturation." *Encyclopedia on Early Childhood Development.* "Immigration." Accessed December 15, 2017. www.child-encyclopedia.com/immigration/according-experts/intergenerational -differences-acculturation.

Canada: Immigration and Refugee Board of Canada. 2014. *Cuba: The musical group "La Opera de la Calle," including information on its members and performances; the closure of El Cabildo Cultural Centre in Havana, including the effects of the closure on the activities of La Opera de la Calle (2012-December 2014).* December 12, 2004. CUB105018.E. Accessed March 22, 2016. http://www.refworld.org/docid/55506ae04 .html.

Capshew, James H. n.d. "Alma Pater: Herman B Wells and the Rise of Indiana University." Accessed March 22, 2016. http://www.indiana.edu/~wells/index.php/archive/the-man -himself/stories/168-story-alma-pater.html.

Klein, Barry, and Beth Kassab. 2000. "The University of Florida's Great Divide." *St. Petersburg Times*, July 2, A1.

Covey, Stephen. 2011. *The 3rd Alternative: Solving Life's Most Difficult Problems.* Free Press.

Dostoyevsky, Fyodor. 1900. *The Brothers Karamazov.* Toronto: New York Modern Library.

Florida Memory. n.d. "Hotel Ta-Miami in Miami." Accessed December 15, 2017. www .floridamemory.com/items/show/268332.

Fowler, Victor. 2016. "Mi [Visita de] Obama." *OnCuba Magazine*, March 16. Accessed March 22, 2016. http://oncubamagazine.com/sociedad/mi-visita-de-obama/.

Goldschein, Eric. 2012. "13 People Who Came To America With Nothing And Made A Fortune." *Business Insider*, February 1. Accessed November 22, 2016. http://www .businessinsider.com/came-to-america-with-nothing-and-made-a-fortune-2012-1#.

González, Gerardo M. 2015. "Give U.S.-Cuba Thaw a Chance." *Huffington Post*, January 25. Accessed March 22, 2016. http://www.huffingtonpost.com/gerardo-m-gonzalez/give -uscuba-thaw-a-chance_b_6548748.html.

González, Gerardo M., and Veronica Kaune Moreno. 1995. "Drug Education in Bolivian Schools: a Feasibility Study for Cross-Cultural Application of a Preventive Curricular Unit." *International Review of Education*, 41 (6): 439–458.

González, Ricardo R. 2015. Dalia Reyes Perera: «Vivo en otras pieles». *Vanguardia*, March 14. Accessed December 15, 2017. http://www.vanguardia.cu/villa-clara/3152-dalia-reyes-perera -vivo-en-otras-pieles?

Hewitt, Keith. 1977. *The Whole College Catalog About Drinking.* Washington: National Institute on Alcohol Abuse and Alcoholism.

Indiana University Bloomington. 2012. "Dean González Receives Honorary Degree from Ivy Tech, Addresses Graduates." *School of Education News*, May 13. Accessed December 15, 2017. http://education.indiana.edu/news/2012-05-13-01.html?

Ingalls, Zoe. 1986. "Alcohol-education Pioneer Tots up a Decade of Success." *The Chronicle of Higher Education*, October 22, 3.

Krull, John. 2014. "Indiana Education Leaders Make Congress Look Good." *The Herald-Times*, July 27.

Pedropan.org. n.d. "The Cuban Children's Exodus." Accessed March 22, 2016. www.pedropan.org/category/history.

Roth, Michael S. 2014. *Beyond the University: Why Liberal Education Matters*. New Haven: Yale University Press.

Sanford, Nevitt. 1967. *Where Colleges Fail: a Study of the Student as a Person*. San Francisco: Jossey-Bass.

Schrecker, Ellen. 1999. "Political Tests for Professors: Academic Freedom During the McCarthy Years." University of California, October 7.

Space War. 2010. "Cuba's Neighborhood Watches: 50 Years of Eyes, Ears." September 27. Accessed March 22, 2016. www.spacewar.com/reports/Cubas_neighborhood_watches_50_years_of_eyes_ears_999.html.

Straus, Robert and Selden D. Bacon. 1953. *Drinking in College*. New Haven: Yale University Press.

Types of Religion. n.d. "Santeria." Accessed March 22, 2016. http://www.typesofreligion.com/santeria.html.

United States Citizenship. 2016. "Inspirational quotes from successful immigrants." Accessed November 22, 2016. https://www.uscitizenship.info/inspirational-immigration-quotes/.

University of Miami Libraries. n.d. "United States. Cuban Refugee Program." Accessed March 22, 2016. http://proust.library.miami.edu/findingaids/?p=creators/creator&id=51.

World Heritage Encyclopedia. n.d. "Little Havana." WHEBN0000896781. Accessed March 22, 2016. www.worldlibrary.org/articles/little_havana.

GERARDO M. GONZÁLEZ, PhD, is dean emeritus of the Indiana University School of Education and professor of educational leadership and policy studies. González has long been a noted and fearless education activist. On his retirement from the deanship in July 2015, he was recognized as one of the thirty most influential deans of education in the United States. In 2017, he was selected to receive one of the most prestigious awards presented by the University of Florida, *The Distinguished Alumnus Award*.